Pearls of Perspicacity

Proven Wisdom to Help You Find Career Satisfaction and Success

> **perspicacity** (pər'spi kas'ə tē) *n.* **1** keen judgment or understanding; acute perception **2** deep vision or insight
> ***SYN***. SHREWDNESS, WISDOM, INSIGHTFULNESS, SHARPNESS, PERCEPTIVENESS, ACUITY, DISCERNMENT.

Dick Lyles

iUniverse, Inc.
New York   Bloomington

Pearls of Perspicacity
Proven Wisdom to Help You Find Career Satisfaction and Success

Copyright © 2010 by Dick Lyles

All rights reserved. No part of this book may be used or reproduced by any means, graphic, electronic, or mechanical, including photocopying, recording, taping or by any information storage retrieval system without the written permission of the publisher except in the case of brief quotations embodied in critical articles and reviews.

The views expressed in this work are solely those of the author and do not necessarily reflect the views of the publisher, and the publisher hereby disclaims any responsibility for them.

iUniverse books may be ordered through booksellers or by contacting:

iUniverse
1663 Liberty Drive
Bloomington, IN 47403
www.iuniverse.com
1-800-Authors (1-800-288-4677)

Because of the dynamic nature of the Internet, any Web addresses or links contained in this book may have changed since publication and may no longer be valid.

ISBN: 978-1-4502-4479-4 (sc)
ISBN: 978-1-4502-4478-7 (dj)
ISBN: 978-1-4502-4477-0 (ebk)

Library of Congress Control Number: 2010932918

Printed in the United States of America

iUniverse rev. date: 8/19/2010

DEDICATION

To my wife, Martha, my love, soul, spiritual guide, and inspiration. I am the most fortunate and most blessed man in the world to have you as my soul mate.

FOREWORD

One of my favorite quotes in the world comes from the writer Samuel Johnson who said, "People need to be reminded more often than they need to be instructed."

I've heard other people capture essential wisdom of that sentiment by saying that there is nothing new under the sun, only new ways to describe old truths. Regardless of how one chooses to say it, the fact is that truth is always precious, whether it is brand new or retold, and the book you are holding in your hands is precious because it is full of truth.

Shortly after being asked to write this foreword, I sat down and read the book for the first time. More important than the way it made me think or feel, it's what it made me do that speaks to its importance—I went to my twelve-year-old twin boys and began to talk to them about it. I shared with them the principles of success contained in the book, principles that if they will embrace now, will serve them for the rest of their lives.

Of course, I am also feeling compelled to practice what Dick Lyles is preaching here. And though I can't say that it is all brand new, the stories he tells and the way he phrases things makes me see these truths in new and compelling ways. And that is often what makes the difference between reading something and agreeing with it, and having it provoke real behavioral change in our lives.

And then there is that word, perspicacity. I like it because it isn't something we read and then quickly dismiss. It makes us wonder why he chose it. And then when we read his explanation, or discover the definition with a few strokes of the keyboard, we remember and retain its meaning because we worked to understand it.

And so it is with this book that Dick has written. In taking the time to read each one-page explanation of the pieces of wisdom contained here, we invest in that wisdom and find ourselves, forty-five seconds later, committed to its truth. So, whether we digest this book in one disciplined reading on a flight across the country, keep it on the nightstand near our bed for occasional extractions, or do something in between, by using it we will be investing in ourselves, in our families, in our organizations, and in our communities. And in the end, we will be making a decision to answer the call of the One who created us to take what He gave us and make something more of ourselves, for others. That's always a good decision.

– Patrick Lencioni
Author of the *New York Times* best-seller *The Five Dysfunctions of a Team*

ACKNOWLEDGEMENTS

This book would never have been written—nor gone into print—without the prodding, inspiration, and encouragement of my wife and toughest critic, Martha.

Our beloved assistant, Marsha Wilson, also deserves a heap of gratitude for having proofed, shaped, and guided the manuscript from idea to printed work.

Thanks to Karen Walker, founder of the CatholicBusinessJournal.biz and producer of my weekly radio show, "The Catholic Business Hour with Dick Lyles." She provided the final impetus to go to press, which was followed by terrific editorial insights and guidance. These gave us a depth of understanding about the material and how to present it that we would not have been able to achieve any other way.

I would be remiss in not also thanking all the people with whom I have worked and come in contact professionally during the past several decades. Each of you contributed in some way to the formulation of these ideas.

Thanks again and Godspeed to each and every one of you!

—Dick Lyles

Contents

DEDICATION v
FOREWORD. vii
ACKNOWLEDGEMENTS. ix
Introduction xiii
Preface: How to Use This Book. xvii
1 Everyone Knows 1
2 The Secret that Will Leverage Your Performance 3
3 One Question that Will Propel your Career to the Stratosphere .5
4 Why Worry about Perceptions?. 7
5 Where to Compete (and Where *Not* to) 11
6 *Who You Are* Doesn't Matter 13
7 Should You Sweat the Small Stuff?. 15
8 The World Isn't a One-Shot World 17
9 The Cold, Hard Facts about "This Vision Thing" 19
10 People Are *Not* Your Organization's Most Important Asset 21
11 Make Your Work a Prayer 23
12 Winners Win with the Hands They're Dealt 25
13 How to Beat the Values Test 27
14 How to Be a Problem-Solving Super Star 29
15 Sharpen Your Judgment by Using Heuristics. 35
16 The Strangest Secret of Personal Power and Influence 41
17 Be a Value-Added Addict. 45
18 Excuses Will Kill You 47
19 Get inside Their Heads 49

20	Power Your Proposals for Success	55
21	Double Your Brain Power	59
22	Only *Your* Name Goes on Your Resumé	63
23	Get Help When You Need It	65
24	Be a Helper	69
25	Use Your Resumé to Manage Your Career	71
26	Achieve Communication Supremacy	73
27	Avoid the Writing Trap	77
28	Leadership Makes a Difference	79
29	Don't Let Others Be Responsible for Your Success	81
30	The Hidden Power of Mentors	83
31	Use Your Self Talk to Your Advantage	85
32	Feedback Is the Breakfast of Champions	91
33	The Most Important Virtue	93
34	Master the Effectiveness Equation	95
35	Be Effectively Flexible	97
36	Don't Let the Past Hold You Back	103
Afterword		109
Bibliography		111

Introduction

For more than three decades I've had the honor of helping improve the performance of executives, managers, supervisors, and individual contributors who work in organizations around the world. To give you a more concrete idea of the variety of these companies, they include Pfizer, Hughes Aircraft, Exxon, Catholic Leadership Institute, Wendy's, TAP Pharmaceutical, and Fidelity National Title in the United States; Ericsson in Sweden; several companies in New Zealand, Australia, and Canada; and the cabinet members and deputies in the Institute of Public Administration in Saudi Arabia, to name a few.

During this time I've learned that the performance effectiveness of any individual is not one-dimensional but instead can be enhanced on a variety of levels. For example, if a person successfully completes a well-structured training program aimed at teaching writing skills, that person will learn to become a more effective and better writer. The same thing can be said for a person learning to become a better communicator, leader, or problem solver. Just about any skill-based competency can be enhanced through effective hands-on training. But skill-based training is not the only way to enhance performance.

One of the most interesting things I've learned is that there exists a large number of truths—fundamental truisms, if you will—that can also serve to enhance an individual's performance and effectiveness in a very tangible and practical way. These aren't the kind of truths that would necessarily be taught in a training program or workshop. But they are nonetheless critical life-truths that people need to know if they want to be successful. Many people learn a large number of these bits of wisdom somewhere along their career path, but many more don't learn or recognize them. And frankly, not everyone has the opportunity to learn them all.

Because I've worked with so many people in so many different career roles, I've been blessed with the opportunity to collect a few more tidbits along the way than most. I've also found myself passing these pearls along to many people through a number of channels: through my consulting and coaching work, my speeches, or my radio show. Yet I've been plagued with the feeling that it isn't enough. Wouldn't it be nice to collect all these insights and worthwhile tidbits of keen insight in one place? My wife and some colleagues agreed. Hence, PEARLS OF PERSPICACITY.

Why "perspicacity," you ask? Why couldn't I just call the book "Pearls of Wisdom"? Or even something more straightforward like "Good Ideas"? The answer is simple. None of those words sufficiently describe the content of the book and the true nature of the ideas presented. Take "wisdom" for example. Wisdom implies a soundness based on knowledge, experience, or understanding that leads to good judgment. Fair enough; the ideas in the book would pass this test. But most of these pearls extend *beyond* mere soundness. So you see, "Pearls of Wisdom" just wouldn't do! It doesn't capture the essence of this content.

Perspicacity, on the other hand, implies a special keenness or acuity applied to insight. It implies a shrewdness, perceptiveness, or acuity that takes the basic notion of wisdom one step deeper. And it is this deeper level of internalization, of living or of "making one's own," of certain truths that I've found gives some people an edge in the career world that others will never even understand, let alone possess.

The most exciting, successful, and fun people I've encountered during my career are also the most perspicacious. They are acutely perceptive well above the norm, have tremendously keen insight, and know how to be effective even when their choices may seem counterintuitive. These perspicacious men and women have the capability to look beyond the obvious, especially when the choices seem intuitively obvious, to find out what will work best, regardless of what others may think or do.

The pearls in this book are some of the most valuable lessons I've culled from these amazing and inspiring individuals along the way. I pass them along to you with best wishes for a fun and fulfilling career from this point forward. It is my most fervent desire that by passing this information along, I'll give you something close to a thirty-year head start toward where you want to go from here. Use these ideas as a foundation to become even more perspicacious during the rest of your career.

May the results of reading these pearls bless not only you, but also ripple out to those hundreds of lives you directly or indirectly impact within your spheres of influence throughout your life!

Dick Lyles

Preface: How to Use This Book

There are numerous ways to take advantage of the ideas presented in this book. One is simply to read it cover to cover. If that's your choice, fine. But I don't think that's the best way to take full advantage of the ideas presented.

Instead I'd like you to consider two other options in order to get more out of this book. Remember, the perspicacious person isn't the one who reads, but is the one who owns—who lives—the truths presented here. So think through these two basic strategies, pick one, and *stick with it*. Either one you pick will make reading the book a more fun, entertaining, and worthwhile experience. Whichever approach you use, be sure to follow through to the end and to apply as many ideas as you can to your life and your career. In other words, make reading about and applying these ideas a game. Just make sure you finish the game with all the points you can.

The first way you might choose to play the game is by yourself—kind of like playing a solitaire card game. This means you would read the chapters, reflect on them, think about how they might apply to you and how you might integrate the ideas into the essence of your being, and experiment with new behaviors based on what you read. After you've finished, you can score yourself to see how many of the ideas you were able to use effectively to improve your career and your life.

The second way to play the game is to go through the book with several other people at the same time. Read each chapter simultaneously, discuss the chapter and what it might mean to each of you, then support each other as you try to implement the changes each person decides to make. Unlike a card game or a game of MONOPOLY® though, you won't be competing with each other. You'll be helping each other as much as possible so you can all "win" together by making these truths an integral part of your lives.

Whether you approach the book individually or with a group, you can either read the chapters in the order they're presented or study them in the sequence of your choosing. The order in which you study each chapter is entirely up to you.

Whichever way you choose, keep two points in mind. First, allow about a week to study, learn, and experiment with the ideas in each chapter. This should take about nine months—the same as a normal school year. Use the week to reflect on the ideas presented, determine whether or not they could make a positive difference in your life, and experiment with new behaviors that will help bring about lasting change in the way you do things.

Second, you should finish *all* the chapters. Whether you take them in the order presented or re-shuffle the order in which you address them, make sure you study them all. Chances are that some of the chapters will address issues that are uncomfortable for you. Other chapters might suggest certain behaviors that don't come naturally to you. That doesn't mean those ideas wouldn't benefit you. It's likely all the ideas will benefit you at least a little, whether they come naturally or not. In fact, some might argue that the suggestions which may benefit you most might be the ones that require the most discomfort on your part to adopt.

So here are the steps you should take to get the most out of this book:

1. Decide whether you're going to read, study, and apply these concepts by yourself or with other people. If you're going to do it with others, recruit them before carrying out the next steps. If you decide to include others, you should include at least two other people but no more than six.
2. Pick one night of the week dedicated to reading, studying, and planning to use the ideas in the book. If you're going to do it by yourself, allow a half hour to an hour. If you're doing it with a group, allow an hour or two. The more people involved, the more time you should allow. You can always adjust these times later if you see fit.

3. Read the selected chapter for that week.
4. Answer the following questions regarding each chapter:
   a. Does this chapter contain knowledge I'm already acting on or have I been acting contrary to these life-truths?
   b. What are specific examples of my behavior that demonstrate that I can and have acted in accordance with these life-truths?
   c. What are specific examples of my behavior that demonstrate I can improve by focusing more on the implementation of these life-truths?
   d. What is my plan for learning more and experimenting with these life-truths this week?
   e. How will I measure success?
   (If you're meeting with a group, each person should share their answers to these questions, and members of the group should ask how they can help each person during the week.)
5. Start the next week's session with a critique of the week's efforts by asking the following questions:
   a. How did you do in comparison to your measures of success?
   b. What did you learn that you didn't expect?
   c. What will it take to successfully implement these ideas?

If you do this each week for a year, there's no question that you'll be a stronger, wiser, and more effective person. "Year?" you say. Wait a minute. There are only 48 chapters and there are 52 weeks in the year!

I know. But I'm assuming you'll take time off for vacation during the year. When that happens, take time off from the book as well. If that number isn't four weeks, say it's three or two weeks off, then guess what? You get to graduate early!

Remember, your goal shouldn't be merely to read through the book. If you plow through it in one setting, it might stimulate your thinking or provide meaningful escape, but it won't lead to the meaningful changes in all the areas that will give you the greatest possible benefit.

Rather, this is a book filled with life-truths to be savored and assimilated into your life. This is the only way to become truly more effective, to dramatically improve your performance, and to become a man or woman of perspicacity. In reading this book, your goal should be to use the ideas presented to help you tangibly develop your potential as much as possible. That will require reflection, thought, planning, and follow-through.

The more effort and time you put into developing yourself in accordance with these ideas, the more you'll benefit. Here's wishing you maximum benefit! Let's begin the journey to perspicacity …

1

Everyone Knows

Don't tell me who you are. Instead let me watch you for a week and I'll tell you. You can't fool people, lie to people, or persuade them to believe something that doesn't match reality for the long term.

Think back to some past jobs you've held or groups of people with whom you've worked. Did you know who contributed and who skated? Did you know who could be trusted and who couldn't? Did you know who could be relied on in a pinch and who couldn't? Did you know who always maintained high standards of performance and who didn't? Did you know who was thorough and responsible and who always looked for the shortcut? Did you know who genuinely cared about the organization and who didn't? Did you know who genuinely cared about other people and who didn't? Did you know who tried to kiss up to the boss and who let their performance speak for itself? Did you know who tried to put a spin on everything so they could take unfair credit and who gave credit where credit was due?

You're darn right you did! But here's the kicker … *so did everyone else!* Some people might be fooled some of the time. Sometimes people say things in public conversations that might seem to indicate that a large number of people are fooled for good. Contrary to such false appearances, however, the reality is that over time everyone knows.

More important, everyone knows about you, or *will know* all about you in time. You can't lie to people about who you are, what you do, or how you act for very long. People who try to live a lie don't last.

This truism demands that we learn two valuable lessons.

The first lesson is: Don't become overly concerned when:

1. You see someone getting away with something you think they shouldn't (such as often slipping out early at the end of the day when the boss isn't looking).
2. You see someone else get credit for work when you think credit should have gone to you or someone else.
3. You think others are getting an unfair share of recognition or appreciation compared to what you deserve.

If you get sidetracked by those concerns, you will pay a price. More importantly, if you embrace those kinds of concerns *and try to act on them,* you'll simply create problems for yourself that you won't want to deal with. In addition, you'll make it harder for people to recognize and act upon your actual performance and the positive contribution you're making.

The second lesson is: Always ensure that your focus is on performing, supporting others in their performance, and working with character and integrity. Why? Because if that's your reality—if that's what's important to you—then over time people will know.

2

The Secret that Will Leverage Your Performance

How you work with people is as important as *what* you do. If you're not seen as someone who is good to be around, a supportive and contributing member of the team, people won't want to be around you. If people don't want to be around you, or don't want you around, you're not going to have much of a career.

The major reason I wrote *WINNING WAYS: Four Secrets for Getting Great Results by Working Well with People* (Putnam, 2000, and Berkley, 2002) was because I had encountered so many people throughout my career who simply didn't understand this important lesson. It breaks my heart year after year to see so many people fall short of realizing their full potential and the full rewards they could accrue because they didn't understand that *the way* they work with other people is critical to their success.

If you are obnoxious, rude, selfish, or abrasive when working with others, it doesn't matter how smart, gifted, or productive you are.

Interestingly enough, the people who don't understand this are also the people who don't realize they are their own worst enemy. I get lots of calls to my radio show, a large number of emails, and frequent questions from people after hearing me speak that go something like this: "I don't think my boss likes me and I don't know why. I do good work and am smarter than most of the people I work with" or "The people I work with aren't very friendly and nice to me. But they all get along and seem to like each other. I don't know why, because I'm probably the best performer in the group."

I have to bite my tongue when I hear statements like these. My impulse is to blurt out, "Can't you see, you poor soul, YOU are the problem—not them!"

People who are insensitive to "process" are likewise insensitive to the impact they have on other people. If everyone else is friendly and respectful with each other and you're the one who's not part of the fun, then chances are that *you* are at least part of the problem, if not all of it. Ask yourself the following questions:

1. Do people often reject my good ideas for reasons that don't make sense to me?
2. Do people seem to cut me out of the conversation when it turns serious and important issues are being discussed?
3. Do the people I work with go to lunch together or spend time during breaks together without including me?
4. Do the people I work with often plan projects and make important decisions without including me when I have knowledge or expertise that could contribute significantly to the work?

If your answer is yes to some or all of these questions, you are probably process-challenged! This means you need to work more effectively with people, taking care how you influence them. You need to pay more attention to *how* you work with people, without compromising your standards or performance. In fact, if you become more process-sensitive in working with others, you'll quickly learn that the overall quality of your work will improve dramatically.

Work well with people and they'll overlook a lot of your sins and shortcomings. Interact poorly with them and it will be almost impossible to sustain lasting achievement.

3

ONE QUESTION THAT WILL PROPEL YOUR CAREER TO THE STRATOSPHERE

Noted management guru Peter Drucker once said that somewhere around 85 percent of the potential to contribute in most management jobs is wasted. Over the years I've shared that observation with many managers. Their first reaction is always similar. "He's crazy," they say. "I put in sixty to seventy hours a week. If anything, I'm working at 150 to 200 percent!"

"Wrong," I say. You see, he didn't say you aren't working hard. Most people work hard. Working hard is not the issue. The issue is how much you contribute to achieving your full potential in whatever position you hold.

Activity doesn't equal productivity.

Most people—especially those in management and leadership positions in organizations—miss most of their potential to contribute in the jobs they hold because they think being busy is the same as being productive. Another reason for missed potential is that they see themselves as caretakers, maintaining continuity, rather than as leaders who are responsible for making things better.

Every job you'll ever hold has tremendous potential for making things better—better for the organization and its people, better for your customers, and better for society in general. It's up to each of us, especially those in leadership positions, to discover the most fruitful ways to make things better and to act on what we find.

The best way to do this is to ask a single question each and every day.

The most valuable and important question you can ask each day is: "What Can I Contribute?"

Many people start their day by asking what they can *get* rather than what they can *give* … to the organization, to colleagues, and to others. Yet the best way to tap into the vast potential of any job you'll ever hold is to ask, "What can I contribute?" Use it as a tool to think about how you can make things better tomorrow than they are today, better than the week before, better than last month, and better next year than last year—for your customers, your co-workers, your company, and the community.

Answer this question wisely, follow up with your answers, and you will create a track record of contribution-oriented achievements that no one will ever be able to take away. "Following up" means being able to look back each month to identify specific contributions you have made to your company, your work environment, or your work to make them better than they were the month before.

You'll spend whatever bonus money you earn. Soon you'll grow tired of the plaques on the wall that cast you in the spotlight for a moment or two. But if you can contribute something special in each job you hold that demonstrates things were better as a result of your efforts, those contributions will stay with you for your entire life.

4

Why Worry about Perceptions?

Regardless of whether other people's perceptions of you are valid or not, they are real. Because they are real to whoever holds them, those people will act on them as if they are real, whether or not they are accurate. The best way to manage perceptions is to perform (see Chapter 1—"Everybody Knows"). Consistently act in a manner that is congruent with the image you want to create in other people's minds, because over time—if given the opportunity—reality will generally win out (see 1 again).

Because people act on their perceptions whether they are valid or not, you owe it to yourself to manage their perceptions of you so you can increase the probability that their perceptions are valid and serve you well. In fact, from time to time it is *essential* that you influence perceptions *for the short term*.

The most important time to manage perceptions is when you are making a first impression. You can only make a first impression once, so it's important that when you make first impressions they are valid and set the proper foundation for your future relationship. Don't go overboard and try to "heap it on" stronger than reality will support. People will see through that. But it's equally important to give thought to your words, your actions, and your personal appearance so that the proper impression is created. A bad first impression will work against you in the long run. You'll have to work three to four times as hard to overcome a bad first impression as you will if you make a good first impression.

Think about how you want others to perceive you in every situation you face. Assess what you say and do to make sure you're acting in a manner that is congruent with this desired perception. Also assess others' perceptions of you to get feedback about how you are perceived compared to how you'd like to be perceived. Then decide what is necessary to bring the two together. You might have to change the way you act or you may have to change the way others think. Usually your strategy will be a combination of both.

A short anecdote underscores the importance of understanding the role of perceptions in on-the-job interactions. One time when I was running a company, two women who worked in the corporate office approached me to complain about the inappropriate behavior of one of the senior male staffers. They alleged that he had repeatedly made statements laden with sexual innuendos and overtones. They said the comments made them so uncomfortable that they didn't want to be near him, let alone work with him. When I told him about the complaints, he erupted. He talked about how close he was to his wife, how many women he'd worked with during his career who could vouch for his fidelity, and how well-respected he was by several prominent women in the company. He said I could rest assured that there were no innuendos and that the negative reaction of these women was inappropriate and out of line.

I asked him if he'd ever received this kind of feedback before. He answered truthfully that it had come up a few times before, but said that in each case, the women were wrong. He said he would never inappropriately approach any woman, and he felt these women had overreacted because of their hang-ups, not his behavior.

It took me awhile to help him understand that if a number of people had reacted the way they did to him, and didn't react that way toward anyone else, then there must be something he was doing to create these perceptions.

At first he was resistant to my suggestion because he felt that if he weren't doing anything wrong and his intentions were noble, then it wasn't fair to ask him to change just to accommodate their false perceptions.

I asked him if he wanted to be perceived as someone who was prone to demonstrate inappropriate behavior. He said he didn't.

I then suggested that if he had noble attentions and wanted to be perceived as such, then it was in his best interest to always act in a way that put him completely above reproach so that he would always be perceived that way in every situation. In other words, his personal knowledge that his intentions were noble wasn't enough. He had to act in such a way that everyone else would perceive him the same way he perceived himself.

Once he adopted this new standard for behavior, no one ever complained about him again. And guess what? General perceptions of his performance and competence improved as well.

5

Where to Compete (and Where Not to)

One of the biggest hindrances to corporate productivity today comes from people within the organization who are *competing against the wrong people*.

First let's talk about who you *should* compete against. The most obvious is people from other companies who are competitors in your marketplace. For example, if you work in a private sector research and development company, you might be competing against universities or some government agencies. In other words, you are in competition with other people who might take away your markets, beat you to market, or in some other way diminish your ability to succeed in your market.

Now let's talk about who you *should never* compete with. First is your boss (or anyone else up the hierarchy). Second, you should never compete with colleagues or co-workers. Third, you should never compete with your subordinates.

But what about people who are in sales positions, you might ask. Aren't they competing with each other to see who can get the most sales, who can be the top performer? The answer is, *they shouldn't be!* If they are competing against each other in win-lose competition (I can win *only if* you lose), then the reward systems are set up wrong. People will put their performance first, *at the expense of everyone else.* They won't pass along leads or, worse yet, will fight over leads and territories and may even sabotage the efforts of other people. Reward systems should be established that will create a win-win culture (I win *only if* you win and we all win together). Under this type of system each person is competing against their own goals for part of the reward and against team goals for additional rewards. An example would be where each person receives half their monthly bonus for achieving their own goals and the remaining half if the team as a whole achieves its team goal.

Whether or not your company's reward systems are designed to create a win-win culture, you should always approach your job with a win-win mind-set. Never put yourself in a win-lose competition with your colleagues, your subordinates, or your boss.

If you compete with your boss or your colleagues, eventually you will lose. Even though the world in which you work may seem cutthroat at times, if you create a competitive dynamic with these people, you will eventually lose out because allies are more important to a successful career than enemies. The same is true for subordinates. You may win a few races here and there because you have the advantage of positional power, but you will lose the war.

Collaborators and coalition builders win in the end. Competition inside the company causes distrust, closed communication, turf-war mind-sets, a "need to cheat" mentality, and backstabbing. Collaboration inside the company causes interdependence, shared responsibility, camaraderie, synergy, consistency, and reliability.

Compete in the marketplace. Compete to win customers, projects, and contracts. But don't compete with your colleagues, co-workers, and those higher up in the hierarchy. Especially don't compete with those below you in the pecking order.

6

WHO YOU ARE *DOESN'T MATTER*

Resumés are indispensable tools insofar as *landing* a job is concerned. However, many people make the mistake of assuming that their resumé (or their background or their educational credentials) should lead to some kind of preferential treatment or special consideration once they're on the job. Not so.

Once you've landed the job, put your resumé away for a while. Forget about *who* you are and all the reasons you should be treated special and start thinking about *how you can contribute* in your new position (see Chapter 3—"The Most Important Question You Should Ask Yourself").

Decision makers—leaders in the organization—don't care who you are (all your credentials, previous honors, academic performance, or what you did for your last employer). The thing that matters most is how well you perform in <u>this</u> job—the quality of contributions you make in <u>this</u> role. No one owes you anything. Past performance means nothing to your current employer if you're not contributing and performing at a high level now.

Celebrate the past, learn from past experience, and use past accomplishments to get your foot in the door. Then lay it to rest and focus on what to do next.

7

SHOULD YOU SWEAT THE SMALL STUFF?

One of the best political campaign consultants I've ever known shared with me a profound insight about political campaign management. She said you always spot the winning and losing campaigns by taking a walk through their campaign headquarters. The winning campaigns are always neat and organized (in sharp contrast to the harried nature of campaigns), the trash is emptied, and there isn't a lot of garbage around. You don't see a lot of half-empty coffee cups and uneaten doughnut pieces that have been lying around for days. Losing campaigns are the opposite. They're staffed by people with holier-than-thou attitudes—people who think they're too important to clean up the mess or do any of the menial tasks.

Once you let the "that's not my job" disease creep into any organization, you're headed down a path toward disaster.

When Delta Airlines was flying high, one of the favorite stories people loved to tell was the story of the Chairman of the Board showing up at the busiest Delta terminal during Thanksgiving week to help with the baggage handling. By demonstrating that no job was beneath him, he set the tone for everyone in the company that they should do what it takes to keep the standards high, regardless of their job description.

The worst thing you can do is think you're "above" doing some task that needs to be done. If something needs to be done and you're in a position to do it (without putting someone else down or stepping on their toes), then do it. And don't look around for a hero's reception.

Don't even worry about whether it will be recognized. Just make a habit of pitching in whenever possible, doing whatever makes sense, and moving along.

Likewise, don't resist a project or an assignment merely because you think it's not big enough, not important enough, or not visible enough. Look at every job as an opportunity to excel and contribute.

Perform well on the little stuff and greater opportunity will find you.

How many times have you heard someone complain by saying, "Gee, you do good work around here and the reward is more work!" Why is this a complaint? Work isn't something we should always think about avoiding. Work is something we should see as an opportunity for true satisfaction and fulfillment. But equally as important, more work is an opportunity to contribute more, achieve more, and ultimately earn more rewards.

If you don't sweat the small stuff, the chances for you and your organization to pursue larger opportunities will be diminished.

After I left the Navy, my very first job had me working for a lousy boss. I was the new kid on the block, and he gave me all the least fulfilling assignments that no one else (including him) wanted. I took on each assignment and did my very best, plus a little extra. Whenever possible I gave him and his department credit for the results that were produced.

Within four to six months he started giving me the best assignments (which typically had the highest visibility to upper management) because he quickly saw it was in his best interest to do so. He could count on my doing an extraordinarily good job, and he didn't see me as someone who was competing with him for the limelight.

The result was that after only fifteen months on the job, he was promoted to a job that was more in line with his competency and didn't involve managing people and I was offered his job. This became one of many instances throughout my career where taking on the menial assignments and doing a good job on the small stuff paid great dividends for me.

8

The World Isn't a One-Shot World

I see it all the time and it drives me nuts. Somebody produces a nice piece of work and then goes bonkers because they didn't get the kind of recognition they thought they deserved for their effort. They act like their whole career and all their life's fulfillment depends upon the honors accorded this single achievement. They try to milk it for all it's worth.

If all you have to offer the world is a single, crowning accomplishment, then give up now.

> ***The world isn't a "one-shot" world—your success will depend on numerous achievements over an extended time period.***

You'll get full credit for some of your achievements, others you won't. Life is fair over the long run (see Chapter 1—"Everyone Knows"), but sometimes it won't seem fair over the short run. The flip side of the coin is that if you stay in the game long enough, there'll be plenty of times you get positive recognition you don't deserve. Recognition is not nearly so important as the accomplishment itself.

This doesn't mean you shouldn't take pride in the work you do or in your accomplishments along the way. Of course you should. But today's great achievement should become a stepping stone for even greater accomplishments tomorrow.

If the world were a one-shot world, meaning if we only had one chance to make our mark, then it might be worth it to fret over each individual accomplishment. Fortunately, however, it's not. This provides two opportunities:

1. An opportunity to move on from opportunities we botch.
2. An opportunity to learn from today's experiences so we can soar to greater heights tomorrow.

9

The Cold, Hard Facts about "This Vision Thing"

If there's one key lesson we've learned about success during the past half century, it's that all meaningful success—either on a corporate level or on an individual level—started with vision.

When we had the big scare back in the early '80s that Japanese companies were going to dominate the world's markets, a number of people studied Japanese companies and concluded that the successful ones—just like successful American companies—all had vision. That was the most important characteristic that differentiated good from bad companies *regardless of whether* the companies were Japanese or American (see *The Art of Japanese Management* by Athos and Pascale).

Simply stated, *every* valid study of organizational leadership conducted during the past five decades has said the same thing:

> ***Vision and purpose are the foundation***
> ***for sustaining organizational excellence.***

Likewise, every valid study of individual human achievement has revealed similar findings on a personal level:

> ***A personal vision and clear sense of personal purpose***
> ***are the foundation for career satisfaction and success.***

The implications are clear. If you don't have a clear personal vision and understand your purpose in life, as well as in each role you fill and in every situation you encounter, **STOP!**

Don't go any further until your aims and intents are clarified.

The same is true for your company (or your department, division, or work group within the company). If the vision and purpose aren't clear, **STOP!**

Don't spend your energy doing anything else until the vision and purpose are clarified.

Otherwise you'll just be going around in circles. How can you measure progress, create alignment, or feel any sense of accomplishment in the absence of a vision?

Vision provides focus. Personal vision dictates the direction you should be moving and guides the way toward personal fulfillment. Organizational vision creates alignment among all the members of the organization.

Vision is the source of the most energy. Human beings are by nature teleological beings. We're the only entities on earth with the capacity to project images of ourselves into the future. When we project those images into the future, it excites and energizes us. Without vision this excitement is lost. Without vision this excitement isn't even possible!

Vision provides accountability. By comparing where we've been and where we are to where we want to be, we can honestly evaluate our progress.

Whether you are thinking about creating a great career, a great company, a great team, or even a great marriage, first think about vision and purpose. Once you've clarified these and obtained commitment from all involved, the sky is the limit. Without clear vision and purpose in place, you don't stand a chance over the long term.

10

PEOPLE ARE NOT YOUR ORGANIZATION'S MOST IMPORTANT ASSET

I recently gave a keynote speech to a group of 500 CEOs. They represented a broad cross-section of industry and companies of all sizes. During my speech I asked, "How many of you think people are your company's most important asset?"

You can probably predict the response. A few hands shot up immediately. Most raised their hands a few seconds later. Finally, those few who didn't totally agree but weren't ready to be seen as politically incorrect raised their hands.

My reply to their response surprised them all. I said, "For those of you who were reluctant to raise your hands, let me tell you I agree. *People are <u>not</u> your organization's most important asset!*"

As you can probably imagine, that statement definitely got their attention. So I repeated it, emphasizing that people are not an organization's most important asset. Some members of the audience got so nervous they started fidgeting in their seats. I knew more than a few were thinking *"Wait a minute, isn't this the leadership speaker? Where's this going?"*

Welcome to the New Economy nestled right in the heart of the Knowledge Age. People aren't assets to your organization. **People <u>are</u> your organization!** That's right, people *are* your organization. Everything else is an asset.

We're not far away from the day when we might even stop referring to people as "Human Resources." You see, that's Old Economy, Industrial Age terminology. The term "human resources" came into being when managers looked around and said, "Well, we have capital resources, financial resources, and … oh, of course, *human* resources."

For those who are skeptical, tell me: Where would your company be *without* people? The answer is simple. You wouldn't have a company. Companies can exist without all kinds of other resources, but they can't exist without people. People *are* your organization and everything else is an asset. So what does this mean?

First, it means that you can't grow your company without growing your people.

Second, it means that if you cheat and undermine your people, you're cheating and undermining your company.

Third, it means that at the end of the day, **it all gets down to people.**

You simply won't be successful for very long if you aren't successful with people. The most valuable competencies you can acquire and demonstrate over time if you want to have a successful and fulfilling career include: the ability to positively influence people, to inspire them, to communicate effectively (both as a leader and a listener), to develop them, and to help them get their needs met in ways that support the accomplishment of your organization's goals.

This is why so many companies are finally waking up to the importance of developing leadership competencies in the ranks of management.

11

MAKE YOUR WORK A PRAYER

Those of us with full-time careers spend more than a fourth of our time each week working. Half the time we're awake we spend at work! It's appalling to me how disrespectful so many of us can be toward this portion of our lives.

Some people see work as a necessary evil. Others see it only as a means to an end (if I didn't have to provide for my economic needs—or for those of my family—I wouldn't work at all). Too few people see work as a noble endeavor that not only satisfies certain unavoidable economic necessities, but also makes a contribution to the world. As a result, our productivity suffers. But more important, people who fail to see the nobility of work suffer from lower self-esteem and lower levels of personal fulfillment than those who recognize the nobility in their work. In addition, those who don't see the nobility of work aren't so healthy, happy, or satisfied with life as people who hold work in higher regard.

Whether or not you're a person of great faith, you will benefit by learning the value of making your work a prayer.

Simply stated, *a prayer is a reverent offering.* Prayers are offered for many reasons, but quite often to pay honored respect.

I believe that our individual talents are God's gift to us. Therefore, what we do with them should be our gift to God.

The more you see your work in this light, the more fulfilled you'll be. You'll be fulfilled because you will perform your work at a higher standard, instill more meaningful value, and carry out all your actions with greater integrity.

It will also cause you to reflect on the service you are providing to others and to society at large through your efforts.

It's certainly desirable to pray in the traditional manner before you go to work and after you get home. But you'll see the greatest elevation of your efforts if you combine work and prayer by making your work a prayer. Make it a reverent offering by using God's grace to mobilize your natural gifts to achieve your unique life's purpose, no matter your job, career, or position.

12

Winners Win with the Hands They're Dealt

Big league baseball pitchers don't win the Cy Young Award for being the best pitcher in their league because they only pitched against the weakest batters during the season or because all the batters they faced decided not to try too hard at the plate.

National Football League teams don't make it to the Super Bowl because they faced all the easiest teams in the playoffs or because the teams they played decided not to try to beat them.

No one accomplishes anything of significance in any field of endeavor because they didn't face any challenges along the way, or because they "got all the breaks," or because everything was handed to them.

People who claim meaningful achievement and success in any endeavor do so because they were effective in dealing with whatever set of circumstances confronted them.

I started out as a freelance, self-employed, independent management consultant at age twenty-six. At about the same time four other colleagues of mine chose the same path. Five years later we attended the same cocktail party and were able to visit and catch up with each other's careers, trials, tribulations, and progress through our individual life's journeys. To my surprise I discovered all four were doing something else. One was selling real estate, one had become a business broker, one went to work for a major corporation, and one was working in government. I was the only one of the five of us who was still doing what we all had started out to do five years earlier.

My conversation with each of them followed an almost identical path. I asked each why he had given up consulting, because I knew each one had held a burning desire to work in that field. Each told me that the desire still existed and that they had loved consulting more than anything they had ever done. However, in each case something had happened to derail them from their goal. They would say, "You're really lucky that this thing that happened to me didn't happen to you and that you made it as a consultant." I didn't have the heart to tell them that in each case, *almost the exact same thing had, indeed, happened to me!* The only major difference is that I was fortunate enough in every instance to find a way around the problem so I could be successful.

Every time you think you've encountered an overwhelming situation, or been dealt a losing hand, I'll bet I can find someone who encountered a similar situation, or worse, and overcame it.

Sometimes in life you'll be dealt situations that are miraculously positive, situations that are so good it would be almost impossible to mess them up. Once in a while you'll be dealt situations that are truly losers, so it's important to be able to recognize the futility of the situation, fold 'em, and move on. But *most* of the time you'll be dealt situations that are challenging yet workable. In those cases your only viable choice is to win. In other words, win with the situations you're dealt.

13

How to Beat the Values Test

Sooner or later … and always more than once … we are all tested. More often than we realize, each of us is put in situations where we are forced to decide what to do based on our values.

After watching hundreds of people put to the test during my several-decades-long career as a consultant and career coach, I've concluded there is only one way to always beat the values test.

The only way to ace the test every time is to clarify your values—decide who you are and what you stand for—*before* you're tested. If you're not going to lie, make up your mind ahead of time. If you're not going to steal, make that decision only once. Then when the test comes, when temptation stares you in the face, you'll pass with flying colors. You won't have to decide *whether or not* you're going to respond to the temptation; you'll only have to figure out how to implement the decision *you already made earlier.*

Invariably, people who struggle the most and often get themselves into trouble with poor decisions are those who believe that their response to different situations should be dictated by the situation rather than by their values. If you put your values first and let them be the determining criteria for your decisions, you'll almost always avoid trouble. If you do the opposite and let the situation determine how you apply your values, you'll get burned most of the time.

That's because temptation is so tempting. If you let the appeal of the temptations guide you instead of deciding beforehand that your values will always be the guiding criteria, your values will lose out. When that happens, you'll almost always regret it later.

If you find yourself saying, "What's the right thing or wrong thing to do here?" in values-loaded situations, then you haven't solidified the appropriate values in your mind in advance. If, on the other hand, you find yourself coming to a conclusion rather quickly about the "rightness" or "wrongness" of certain decisions, and are merely struggling with the best way to implement your conclusions, then you are going to avoid a lot of heartburn in this area.

Later on in life you'll be able to sleep tight at night and look yourself in the mirror in the morning, finding comfort in the knowledge that you were true to yourself and your values when put to the test. There will be great satisfaction in looking back and knowing you passed the values tests in flying colors when they were put to you.

14

How to Be a Problem-Solving Super Star

Whoever sees the problem has the responsibility to *see to it* that the problem is solved. You may not be the person who ultimately solves it because the solution may lie outside the boundaries of your personal responsibilities. But regardless of whether the problem is yours to solve, if you see that it's creating a negative impact on the organization, then you *must* see to it that whoever is responsible solves the problem.

In order to either solve problems or see to it that problems are solved, it's important to understand problem solving.

During your career you've probably encountered a number of different approaches toward organizational problem solving. I propose you learn and use the Lyles Seven-Step Method which has been taught in twelve languages to more than 50,000 people in twenty-two countries on six continents. Its steps include:

1. Define the Problem
2. Define Objective(s)
3. Generate Alternatives
4. Develop Action Plan
5. Troubleshoot
6. Communicate
7. Implement

Here's a closer look at each of the seven steps:

Define the Problem

The first step in problem solving is to understand what the problem is and to define the problem clearly so that others can also understand what it is. In organizations, problems are either obstacles or deviations. An obstacle prevents the outcome you desire. A deviation is a different outcome than you desire. A problem has both a cause and an effect. Logic tells me that if something is happening other than what I want to happen, then something had to have happened to cause the different outcome. I don't understand the problem unless I understand both the undesired effect *and* what caused it. A simple definition of a problem might follow this general format:

A (something)
is causing
B (some undesirable effect).

Following this format, a specific problem might be clearly defined as:

Fred's continual failure to submit information promptly to me
is causing
me to finish and file my reports late.

To check your definition of a problem, be sure that it describes both a cause and an effect. Remember that the definition of a problem describes only an undesirable effect and its cause—the definition doesn't imply solutions.

Define Objective(s)

The second step is to define objectives—define the outcome you would like to achieve as a result of solving the problem.

Objectives specify only the outcome you would like to achieve. The action plan, which is developed in step four, specifies the means by which you hope to achieve this outcome. An objective might follow this format:

To ensure that *actor*
performs *action*
by *date*
at *cost.*

Following this format, a clear definition of objectives for the specific problem with Fred might read:

To ensure that *Fred*
submits the information I need
by *the 10th of each month*
at *no additional cost.*

To ensure that *I*
submit my reports
by *the 15th of each month*
at *no additional cost.*

Of course, the number and format of objectives may vary according to the definition of the problem you are trying to identify and your priorities, but you will find this simple format a good starting point.

GENERATE ALTERNATIVES

This is the solution-generating step of the process. In this step you generate as many alternative solutions possible to achieve the objectives you defined in the previous step. For example, if you were to generate alternative ways to solve the problem with Fred, you might compile a list such as this one:

- Discuss the problem with Fred
- Discuss the problem with my boss
- Discuss the problem with Fred's boss
- Write Fred a memo asking for his cooperation
- Ask for a transfer
- Reorganize so I don't have to rely on Fred
- Ask that Fred be transferred
- Ask that Fred be fired

- Do nothing
- Submit the reports without Fred's input, stating the reason was his failure to cooperate
- Submit a written complaint to Fred's department head
- Submit a written complaint to my boss
- Threaten Fred
- Resign

Some of these alternatives are not good ones. However, at this point, generating as many alternatives as you can is useful because some that aren't good may lead you to others that are. Remember that in this step you are only generating alternatives—not evaluating them or selecting them.

DEVELOP ACTION PLAN

This step has two phases. First, evaluate the alternatives you generated in the previous step and choose one or more as your solution. Second, modify the chosen alternative(s) until an action plan is fully developed.

An outline of a very simple action plan that might be used in the early stages of Fred's problem could include the following:

1. Talk to my boss first; explain my problem with Fred and what I intend to do about it
2. Talk to Fred, addressing the following:
    - The impact of his behavior on me
    - The impact of his behavior on the organization
    - The desired behavior
    - The consequences of not changing his actions
    - The consequences of acting as desired
3. Report the results of my conversation with Fred to my boss
4. Provide Fred with performance-based feedback regarding his subsequent behavior

TROUBLESHOOT

Most problems are the result of solutions. The best way to avoid these additional, unintended problems is to troubleshoot your action plan before you implement it.

Troubleshooting the action plan is the most cost-effective and efficient problem solving you can perform.

Review your action plan in terms of the future and try to anticipate potential problems. Then modify your action plan to solve these problems or to bypass them before they occur or before they become potential crises.

In troubleshooting your action plan for the problem with Fred, you might anticipate some of these potential problems:

1. Fred may not respond to your discussion
2. Fred may go to his department head and complain that you are harassing him
3. Your boss may tell you to leave Fred alone

You can think of other potential problems. As the problem solver, you must decide which of these are serious enough to warrant your modifying the action plan. For those that are less serious, you may simply develop contingency plans.

COMMUNICATE

In this step determine which individuals or groups might affect the success of your action plan. Then determine the best method for giving them the best information to ensure the success of your action plan. You can choose from many methods of communicating to these people the information you want them to have; for example, personal visits, telephone calls, memos, letters, audio tapes, videotapes, and computer messages.

For people, you specify different communication objectives. For the problem with Fred, you might outline a simple plan such as this:

PERSON	OBJECTIVE	METHOD
My Boss	Seek Advice Gain Support	Personal Visit
Fred	Change Behavior Meet Deadlines Seek Future Cooperation	Personal Visit

IMPLEMENT

This final step in problem solving involves more than merely *starting* the action. You haven't solved a problem until you have achieved *all* the objectives you have defined. Therefore, implementation involves follow-up and monitoring through the completion of every objective your action plan specifies.

In the case of the problem with Fred, *starting* the action is simple. But following up and monitoring Fred's behavior will be an important part of implementation.

If you see a problem that someone else has the responsibility to solve, you'll be more helpful to the problem solver if you define the problem using one of the formats shown earlier. If you are the problem solver, then you'll want to develop the habit of using all seven steps yourself. Sometimes you'll zip through the steps in a matter of minutes. For more serious problems you might take days, weeks, or even months to complete all seven steps. The important thing to remember is to follow the seven steps in order, finishing the work completely with each step before going to the next.

Use this tool effectively and you'll definitely become a problem-solving super star which, in turn, will enhance your value to your organization and to the job market at large.

15

Sharpen Your Judgment by Using Heuristics

What are heuristics? Heuristics are mental shortcuts we use to simplify judgments we make about complex issues. In essence, they are mental rules of thumb we use to sort through complex loads of data so we can make judgments that will lead to decisions.

Some heuristics are helpful, some are not. Sometimes heuristics lead us quickly to accurate judgment, other times they lead to either partial or complete and often permanent misunderstanding. Racial stereotyping is an example of one kind of negative heuristic that is more damaging than helpful.

Experience can be one of the best teachers, but only if we learn the right thing from our experiences. Improperly relied upon, heuristics can cause people to learn the wrong lessons from their experiences.

Consider the following story told by Daniel Kahneman about his experience teaching flight instructors to be better trainers.

As a junior professor, Kahneman was teaching a course in the psychology of training to a group of Air Force flight instructors. He explained that positive reinforcement and rewards were more effective training tools than punishment or negative reinforcement. He cited the work of several behavior modification theorists, including B.F. Skinner and his efforts to prove these theories by working with pigeons. One of the flight instructors challenged him by claiming just the opposite. The objecting flight instructor explained that he had often praised people warmly for beautifully executed maneuvers only to see the pilots do worse on their next attempt. He had also screamed at pilots for badly executed maneuvers and then seen them improve.[1]

After reflecting for a moment, Kahneman realized that this was an example of Sir Francis Galton's statistical principle referred to as the "theory of regression toward the mean." This principle says that in any series of somewhat random events clustering around a mean, or average, that an extraordinary event (which is far from the mean) is more likely to be followed by a more ordinary (closer to the mean) event. That is to say the student pilots were improving their mean level of performance so slowly that the instructors weren't consciously noting the changes in the mean performance level! These changes occurred almost imperceptibly over time. The differences in variations that were occurring on either side of the mean, however, were what the instructors noticed as the mean improved.

Put simply, odds are always that a student pilot who makes a three-point landing today will not perform that well (at the same level) tomorrow, regardless of whether today's landing is followed by praise or punishment.[2] The same is true when a student performs extraordinarily poorly. The poorer the performance—in other words, the greater the deviation from the mean—the greater the likelihood that the student will perform better on the next attempt.

There are two different heuristics at work here, and it is important to understand the difference in order to sharpen your judgment. Let me explain.

First is the *representative heuristic*. The representative heuristic involves taking a sample of the data and automatically inferring that the sample is representative of the whole, regardless of whether or not this is true. In the case above, it is not true. The objecting flight instructors recalled only the most extraordinary events, all of which were likely to be followed by more ordinary events. They then drew the wrong conclusions about positive and negative reinforcement. If they had tracked the mean performance level instead, they would have learned the truth. Positive reinforcement leads to improvements (positive changes in the mean performance level) over time, while negative or no reinforcement leads to lower or no gains in performance over time.

---

1   Kevin McKean, "Decisions, Decisions," *Discover* (June 1985): 22-31.
2   Ibid.

The second kind of heuristic that came into play in this example is the *co-variation heuristic*. The co-variation exists when a person attributes causality that doesn't actually exist. In other words, a person may assume a cause and effect relationship to exist between events, but that assumption is not true. In our example above, the objecting flight instructors witnessed extraordinarily good performance followed by praising, followed by merely ordinary performance. The instructors concluded that the praising caused the pilots' performance to decline. But the true odds are that the performance would have gone down anyway, whether or not the pilots received praise after their first "extraordinary" performance. Likewise the objecting instructors saw extraordinarily bad performance followed by screaming, followed by better performance, and wrongly concluded the screaming caused the performance to improve. It's much more likely the performance would have improved for that exercise regardless of the screaming.

We can learn a valuable lesson from the experience of the flight instructors: *How easy it is to learn the wrong lessons from your experiences!*

The flight instructors witnessed events with 100 percent accuracy. Yet they came to exactly the wrong conclusion. They concluded that praising leads to decline in performance and punishment leads to improvements, when exactly the opposite is true! How many people have you seen during your life who have learned this same lesson incorrectly? Teachers? Coaches? Parents? Grandparents? Supervisors? Make sure that when you chalk up your learning to experience, you're learning the right lessons.

Another heuristic that will play an important role in your career is the *framing heuristic*. The framing heuristic allows you to influence people's judgment (including your own) simply by the way you state the problem. I love to pose the following dilemma to participants in many of the workshops I conduct. I ask them to quickly answer "yes" or "no" to the following two scenarios developed by Kahneman and his colleague, Amos Tversky. Try it for yourself. Here are two scenarios I often present. Quickly answer "yes" or "no" to each one:

> You've decided to see a Broadway play and purchased a $75 ticket. As you enter the theater, you realize that you've lost your ticket. You can't remember the seat number, so you can't prove to management that you bought a ticket. Would you spend $75 for a new ticket?
> Yes _____ No _____
>
> You've reserved a seat for a Broadway play for which the ticket price is $75. As you enter the theater to buy your ticket, you discover you've lost $75 from your pocket. Would you still buy the ticket? (Assume you still have enough cash left to do so.)[3]
> Yes _____ No _____

Typically about 60 to 80 percent of the people give a different answer to the two questions. The most common response is to say "no" to the first question and "yes" to the second. Most people will buy a ticket after losing the cash, but won't buy one after losing the ticket. Why?

"Our story is that you set up a mental account for going to the theater and, in the first problem, have already charged it [$75]," says Tversky. "If you buy another ticket, your theater account now doubles, perhaps more than you're willing to spend. But in the second problem, you merely charge the loss to some other mental account. You can take it out of next month's lunch money or next year's vacation."[4]

What about people who answer both questions the same? They framed the two situations differently.

Different people frame different situations differently based on their values, principles, experiences, education, and priorities at the moment. However, we can influence the framing process of another individual based on how we present certain ideas, proposals, or solutions to problems (see Chapter 17—"How to Frame Your Proposals for Success").

The best way to frame a proposal is using the Seven-Step Method presented in Chapter 14.

---

3   Ibid., 29.
4   Ibid., 30.

Many people submit their proposals as a proposal to *do* something rather than as a proposal to *solve a problem.* Yet the first proposal approach is more likely to create resistance from the outset. For example, a proposal to "Purchase new Photocopying Equipment" is much less likely to be embraced from the outset than a proposal to "Solve the Photocopying Problem" in our corporate region.

When you start by saying, "We need to do this," most people's natural reaction is to push back. They want to know why, what can be gained, and who said we need to.

Instead start a proposal by defining a problem and gaining agreement that there is a problem. Most people will respond by saying, "What should we do about it?" or "How should we solve it?" This is a much more open and receptive frame of mind from which to proceed.

If you use the Seven-Step Method as an outline for your proposal, you will create a problem-solving mental framework in other people that is conducive to achieving understanding and positive action.

16

The Strangest Secret of Personal Power and Influence

Do this: Close your eyes for a moment. What words come to mind, what words do you associate with the word "power"? You can also play this game with a few other people if you want to confirm your reactions.

I've played this game with dozens of groups of people during workshops and seminars I've conducted throughout my career, and the responses are always similar. People most often think of words such as control, coerce, authority, rule, command, clout, domination. What's interesting about these words is that for the most part they have a negative connotation. Very rarely do people come up with positive word associations for power.

To a large extent these negative associations stem from widely held views in society that the exercise of power in interpersonal relationships is negative and that people who seek power are viewed negatively. People are suspicious of people who want power. Most important, people might even question their own motives if they seek power, not wanting to be seen as seeking power to exploit others.

But there is another, more positive way to view power.

Perhaps one of the all-time classic pieces regarding interpersonal power and influence is presented in an article entitled "The Two Faces of Power," by David C. McClelland.[5]

---

[5] David C. McClelland, "The Two Faces of Power," *Journal of International Affairs* 24, no. 1, reprinted in *Organizational Psychology, A Book of Readings,* David A. Kolb, et al. (Upper Saddle River, NJ: Prentice Hall, 1971).

In this article McClelland examines some of the traditional, negative connotations of power. At the same time he reveals a more positive, nontraditional view that allows us to view power through a completely different perspective.

McClelland says the negative face of power is only part of the story. The positive face is the other part. Our challenge, he says, is to try to understand both faces. When is power good and when is it bad? Why is it often perceived as dangerous? When is it right and when is it wrong to try to influence others? How do we use our interpersonal power most effectively?

Let's first look more specifically at the two faces of power. McClelland describes one face as an unsocialized concern for personal dominance. The other face is more socialized and is concerned more with inspiring people in order to win an objective or achieve a common goal.

In his article, McClelland cites a study in which a group of students were shown a film of John F. Kennedy's "New Frontier" inaugural address. A control group was shown a film about modern architecture. Afterward both groups were tested to see if the films changed any of their fundamental attitudes about themselves. There were no changes in the students who watched the architecture film. But the changes in the students who watched the Kennedy film were profound. There was an increase in their feelings of personal power. They clearly felt strengthened and uplifted by the experience. They felt more powerful, rather than less powerful and submissive.

What is most interesting in this finding is that it challenges the traditional way of explaining the influence that effective leaders have on their followers. Leaders such as Kennedy *do not* force followers into submission and followership by the overwhelming magic of their personalities and their persuasive powers. Rather, they are effective by strengthening and inspiring potential followers.

This gets at the true second face of power. Leaders who rely on the positive face of power arouse confidence in their followers. They make followers feel stronger, rather than weaker, as a result of their interactions. Never should the leader think of their role as one that forces people into submission. To the contrary, the role of a leader should be to strengthen people, uplift them, and turn them into self leaders. As

President Kennedy demonstrated, *when using this approach, the more power a leader gives, the more power the leader will get in return.*

According to McClelland a leader's message should not so much be: "Do as I say because I am strong and I know what's best for you," but "Here are the goals which are true and right and which we share. Here's how we can reach them. You are strong and capable. You can accomplish these goals." Thus the leader's role is to articulate a vision, clarify goals, and then create confidence that the followers can achieve them. This is true in relationships that are both hierarchical and collegial. In other words, this should be someone's approach regardless of whether they are talking to direct reports, peers, colleagues, or people higher up in the chain of command.

This leads us to both the ultimate paradox of social leadership and the strangest secret of interpersonal power and influence: To be an effective leader, you must turn all your so-called followers into leaders!

17

Be a Value-Added Addict

A lesson we teach kids in sports is to be always "first on and last off." In other words, show up to practice early and work late to develop your skills and prepare for the real contest.

It's also a lesson that carries over into our careers. One of the best habits you can develop is to be first on and last off to work every day. But a big difference you should make in applying this concept to work is to realize that we're not just talking about when we punch the clock. We're also talking about the *value* we add to everyone's effort through our own extra effort.

In my book, *WINNING HABITS: Four Secrets that Will Change the Rest of Your Life* (Financial Times Prentice Hall, 2004), I tell the story of Albert, who was stymied in his career until he started adding value to every project to which he was assigned. Once this became a habit for him, his career took off.

The same could easily happen to you.

Adopt an attitude that instead of merely meeting the requirements of different tasks that are assigned to you, you *always* look for a way to do just a little bit extra or carry out your work in such a way that you clearly add value over and above what is expected. You will be amazed at the impact this will have on how you are perceived by others and how it will affect your career. Opportunities will come knocking that you would never have been exposed to otherwise.

Keep in mind two cautions when you follow this advice, however. First, every project reaches what can be referred to as the "good idea cut-off point." You've reached this point when you've worked the problem to the point where new suggestions don't add true value—all they do is give more people "ownership" or an opportunity to say they participated. It's time then to cut off any further debate or dialogue and move forward with what you've developed so far.

The second caution is not to be flippant when you're thinking of adding value. Don't just throw out ideas to see if they'll stick so that you can say some of your ideas have been included. Instead only bring forth proposals and suggestions that you have thought through and that are sure to make an improvement in efficiency, effectiveness, or outcomes.

A final point to remember is that when you adopt the "first on and last off" mind-set, make sure you are spending the extra time and energy wisely. Use the extra time to make a significant positive difference. I once worked with a CEO who had a department head who would stay at work late a couple of times of week. The department head would always make it a point to call the CEO on his cell phone during these times. When the CEO would ask him what he was working on, it was always something that wasn't that important. The CEO quickly surmised that this guy was only trying to impress him and really wasn't all that productive (see Chapter 1—"Everyone Knows"). The point is to implement "first on and last off," as well as all these other recommendations, with a clear and noble purpose, and not just to be noticed or to give a false impression to others.

18

Excuses Will Kill You

When I was a plebe at the Naval Academy at Annapolis, we had to learn to live by many stringent rules, but one in particular has proven to be a lifesaver to me throughout my career. It's saved a lot of others who live by it as well. The rule was nonnegotiable: "No excuse, Sir!"

During our plebe year hazing we were told to do a number of things. At every meal we'd sit at tables with four plebes and eight upperclassmen. The upperclassmen would fire questions at the plebes. Most of the questions focused on things we didn't know. We could never respond by saying, "I don't know." Nor could we guess. If we didn't know the answer, we had to respond by saying, "I'll find out, Sir."

We had to find answers to all the questions we didn't know by the next meal, or we'd have hell to pay. Invariably, we'd forget a question or not be able to find the answer in the time allotted. But the upperclassmen never forgot. So when they asked the question again at the next meal and we didn't know the answer, we'd again say, "I'll find out, Sir."

They'd respond by reminding us that that's what we'd said during the last meal. Then they'd drill us: "So why didn't you find out?" No matter how good your reasons were, you could never give an excuse. The only acceptable response was, "There's no excuse, Sir."

Some people hear about this and their first reaction is that it sounds unfair. At first it sure seemed that way to us plebes too!

But after a while we realized that excuses are nothing more than a justification or explanation. If you commit to something, you should do it. Your standard for letting yourself off the hook should be high—not something you let go of lightly with some simple rationalization.

People who let excuses rule their lives never reach the top. Successful people meet their commitments no matter what obstacles stand in their way.

It might be helpful to reflect on how many times you haven't done something you said you'd do. How many times did you use some flimsy excuse as an out? Then reflect on whether or not you actually could have delivered what you promised if you'd been more alert or managed your time better. Usually you'll find you could have done so.

Remember that when all is said and done, if you don't get the job done, the excuses don't matter. All the excuses in the world don't matter. The fact is that you failed to achieve what you set out to do. Excuses are never a substitute for results.

Results are all that count. Never accept an excuse for falling short.

19

GET INSIDE THEIR HEADS

Milton Ericson is to hypnotherapy what Sigmund Freud is to psychotherapy. Ericson was without a doubt one of the foremost hypnotists in history, if not the all-time best. He accomplished amazing feats working with patients by accessing their subconscious minds (getting inside their heads, if you will) and working with them to overcome various mental maladies.

One of his great challenges, however, was that Ericson couldn't describe or teach his methods to others. He knew his approach worked. He knew how to make it work when working with patients. But he couldn't teach others how to perform his seemingly magical feats of hypnosis, hypnotherapy, and influence.

Along came a couple of Ericson's students, Richard Bandler and John Grinder. They spent ten years studying the hypnotic techniques of Ericson with phenomenal results. Their findings were published in a two-volume work entitled *The Structure of Magic (Volumes I and II)*.[6] The two books documented the methods behind Ericson's "magic" by describing in detail the methods and practices Ericson used to access the subconscious thought processes of his subjects.

Since reading these two works in the late 1970s I've had the opportunity to observe a large number of consultants, executives, managers, supervisors, coaches, salespeople, and people in a wide variety

---

6   Richard Bandler and John Grinder, *The Structure of Magic, Vols. 1 and 2*. (Palo Alto, CA: Science and Behavior Books, 1975 and 1976).

of other leadership positions and have found that the most influential of these people use many of the same techniques. They very subtly but skillfully get inside the heads of the people they influence to enhance their power of influence proportionately. People in those same roles who don't use these techniques are much less influential and less effective.

My experience has revealed that three of these techniques are used far more often than the others among the most influential people I've worked with. These are: 1) harmonizing the interaction, 2) framing the focus, and 3) using stories to persuade.

Harmonizing the Interaction

The most powerful people I've worked with take the time to connect with the people they will influence before actually attempting to influence them. They realize that *how* things are said is every bit as important as *what* is said. They operate on the implicit understanding that unless they connect by creating a resonating harmony with the people they want to influence, they are stacking the deck against themselves.

Powerful influencers will match the voice tones, volume, speech rate, and rhythms of those they want to influence. The very best will even go so far as to match the other person's body language, posture, and mood. They will also match the style of language the other person is using by matching predicates. For example, if the person uses visual predicates such as "I see" or "I can't picture that," the most powerful influencers will respond by saying "Let me show you," as opposed to "let me explain," the latter predicate being more audio than visual. On the other hand if the person says, "I don't understand," the influencer will very likely respond by asking him to explain in more detail. Overall, the influencer functions almost as a highly sensitive biofeedback mechanism, reflecting and sharing the other person's present reality. The best influencers sometimes get to the point where they are breathing in and out with the other person!

Another technique that powerful influencers use to establish harmony is called "pacing." Pacing falls into two categories: descriptive and objective.

Descriptive pacing involves the use of patently true pacing statements that create a feeling of trust and rapport in the mind of the listener. "You said you have another meeting at three o'clock." "It's been rainy these past few days, hasn't it?" Statements like these create a mind-set of agreement and help establish an unconscious affinity between influencer and responder. Inexperienced and less effective influencers tend to jump right in and start trying to persuade. Because they haven't established a subconscious bond, their results suffer accordingly.

Objective pacing involves responding to an objection with agreement, then leading the responder in a direction that undermines the objection. A direct report tells the supervisor, "This is going to be challenging for our people. I don't know if we have enough people or enough time to get this accomplished." The supervisor responds, "I agree, it is going to be a major challenge, but it will benefit the company and our people in several important ways." Then the supervisor delineates the benefits of the proposal, usually with a positive response. Less effective influencers try to meet objections directly—they argue whether or not the objections are valid. The result is resistance and uncooperativeness, which leads to poorer results.

The more you can do to get in harmony and stay in harmony with people during your interactions, the more effective you'll be in the long run.

FRAMING THE FOCUS

Once a bond of trust and rapport is created, the next step is to frame the focus of the interaction by using suggestions and indirect commands that begin to lead the other person in the direction the influencer wants to go.

One way to start framing the focus is to use descriptive pacing statements as bridges to influencing or to use leading statements. "Our total budget this year is ten million dollars. One of the areas in which we need to make significant progress is in the goals we've set for this project." It doesn't matter whether there is a connection between the pacing and the leading statement. These can be entirely unrelated. What happens, however, is that the first patently true pacing statement creates an affirmative frame of mind. When that framework of agreement is established, it is almost impossible for the responder to change to a negative frame of mind or a mind-set of disagreement when he processes the next sentence. Therefore, agreement is almost guaranteed.

People who agree with people unconsciously expect further agreement. People who start out disagreeing with people expect further disagreements. The most effective people thus start out with agreeable pacing statements, then use more pacing statements to build bridges to framing statements that help focus the listener in the direction of the desired action. As this happens, the responder takes more and more of what the influencer says as both factual and personally significant.

The next step is to use a language structure referred to as an "imbedded command." An imbedded command is nothing more than a command imbedded in a larger statement that on the surface may seem somewhat innocuous. "I'm going to share an idea with you that will cause you, Bob, *to put your very best energy and efforts into achieving these goals.*" Placing the person's name just before or just after the imbedded command makes it more powerful. The most effective influencers pause before the command, then change rhythm, volume, and tone of their speech when delivering the command to add still more power. Used properly, these imbedded commands are hard to resist.

A final step in the process of helping to frame the focus is to use *factive presuppositions*. These statements require the listener to first accept some other supposition as factual in order to respond affirmatively to what is stated next. A good prosecuting attorney, for example, doesn't say to the jury, "Your job is to determine whether the defendant committed this crime." The best prosecutors will say instead, "Your job is to determine why the defendant committed this crime." The jurors can't reasonably ask why the defendant committed the crime unless they have first accepted the presupposition that the defendant did, in fact, commit the crime. Once they've accepted that fact, the prosecutor has won the case.

I used a more positive example when I coached kids in sports. After they'd make a good play or perform well in some respect I'd ask, "How does it feel to be such a good player?" or "What's it feel like to perform so well?" It didn't matter how they responded to my question. More important was that in order to answer the question, the young ball player had to accept as fact (on a subconscious level) the presupposition that they were, in fact, a good player or a good performer. Think of how different it would have been if I had told an eleven- or a fourteen-year-old, "You're a good player." Most often the response to such a direct assertion is negative. Kids answer, at least in their own minds (which gets programmed into their subconscious) with statements like, "I'm not that good," or "I'm not as good as Sally."

Using the factive presupposition in a coaching situation programs the learner's subconscious to accept the positive premise *as fact*. Another tool that helps people accept your statements as true is storytelling.

Using Stories to Persuade

Throughout history people have influenced, guided, and inspired others with anecdotes, parables, metaphors, and short stories. It was one of Ronald Reagan's strengths as a leader. Every speech he gave included short stories and anecdotes that aroused interest, built trust and rapport, and even delivered information about his intentions. Information that otherwise might be dry and dull can take on an energy of its own and—perhaps even more important—take on a human dimension, when delivered via story or metaphor.

Here are some examples: "I tried this with another client of mine in a similar industry, and what worked best was that it involved everyone in operations and created an alignment they hadn't seen in years." "It's kind of like distinguishing between fleas and elephants. The elephant represents the results you'll get following this approach, and the fleas are all the little implementation concerns you'll have to work through to get there." Very quickly these statements frame the issue in a perspective that's helpful to the persuader. This approach makes it easier for another person to grasp your point. Yet it is done indirectly, bypassing direct arguments and intellectual tugs-of-war that could drain energy and slow progress.

At first when you try these techniques, they'll seem clumsy and awkward, the same as when you try any new skill. The more you use them, however, the smoother you'll become and the more quickly you'll see improved results. Most importantly, though, your effectiveness as an influencer will improve as you become more adept at getting inside people's minds without having to kick down doors and windows.

20

POWER YOUR PROPOSALS FOR SUCCESS

Marketing experts and people who specialize in the creation of advertising media have learned an important lesson about how people process information in ways that lead to action.

They've learned that in order to get people to act in a certain way in response to advertising communication, they must process the advertiser's message through five levels of information processing. These five levels are unawareness, awareness, understanding, commitment, and action (see Figure 20.1).

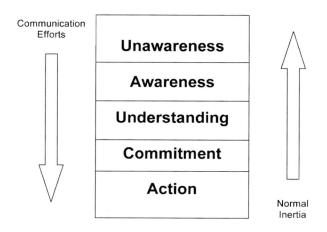

Figure 20.1 Levels of Information Processing

If the communicator wants a person to take a specific action, the message must be constructed in such a way that it is able to penetrate through each level of another person's information processing to ultimately bring about the desired action. Normal inertia, background noise, and various other factors will work against the communicator's ability to achieve this objective.

Consider the advertiser who is creating a full-page magazine ad. Because the ad has to compete with at least dozens and maybe hundreds of other ads and messages, the advertiser must first get the reader's attention. This is so important that advertisers typically spend from two-thirds or more of their budget and advertising space on a picture or image that will entice and draw the reader to the ad and pique the reader's attention.

The advertiser realizes, however, that attention alone does not necessarily lead to understanding. So the headline in the full-page ad is carefully written to further catch a viewer's interest and communicate the compelling benefits to the viewer if he reads more.

The text in the ad then takes the reader from understanding to commitment—*commitment in the mind of the reader*. Words like "Imagine yourself driving down the road, surrounded in the comfort and satisfaction of knowing this car was built just for you" build commitment and motivation to act. Then there's usually some triggering mechanism—what is often referred to as a "call to action"—such as "Stop by and test drive one today" or "Go see your nearest dealer right now."

The biggest problem most people make when writing or presenting proposals in organizations is that they jump from the first step (unawareness) to the last step (action), and skip everything in between. In effect, they barge in and say, "Here's what we need to do." The result is resistance because the proposal hasn't been framed properly to lead and enable others to support it (see Chapter 15—"Sharpen Your Judgment Using Heuristics").

Use the Seven-Step Method to frame your proposals, and you will create a strong, positive framing process as well. Study Figure 20.2.

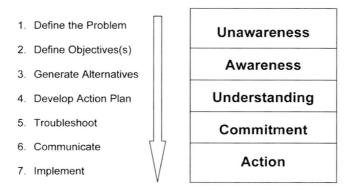

Figure 20.2 Problem-Solving Steps as Framework for Communicating

Although it is not a one-to-one correlation, it is easy to see that defining the problem and defining objectives help to penetrate the barriers of unawareness and awareness. Generating alternatives, developing action plan, troubleshooting, and communicating help to work through the barriers of understanding in order to gain commitment. And finally, commitment to implementation leads to taking action.

Let me tell you about a terrific aha! moment one of my executive trainees experienced. A few years ago I was teaching problem solving and decision making to a group of senior executives in Sydney, Australia. I had just finished presenting these ideas when one of the executives, Geoffrey, slammed his pen down on the table and exclaimed, "I don't believe it!"

A bit surprised, I stepped back and said, "What is it you don't believe?"

"For thirteen years I've been with this company and for thirteen years I've been doing it wrong! I can't believe all the nightmares I've created for myself."

I paused for a moment, then asked, "What have you been doing wrong?"

"This!" replied Geoffrey passionately. "Every time I've ever submitted a proposal, I've always submitted it as a proposal *to do something*. I submit the proposal and then spend the next six months to a year trying to defend it. Sometimes I'm successful, sometimes I'm not. But it always turns out to be major battle. In fact, I have just such a proposal on my desk right now. It's a proposal to our headquarters in New York to purchase new photocopying equipment for the Australasia region. The proposal is complete, but I haven't sent it in yet because I don't want to start the battle I know I'll have to fight."

We discussed his situation for a few minutes and talked about how to properly frame the proposal. Upon completion of the workshop I returned to San Diego and he went back to work.

Ten days later I received a call from him in Sydney. "Dick, Geoffrey here."

"Hey, Geoffrey, what's up?"

"You're not going to believe this. It's so incredible I just had to ring you up. I rewrote the proposal we discussed. Instead of making it a proposal to purchase new photocopying equipment for the region, I wrote it as a proposal to solve the photocopying problem we have in the region. I started by explaining the problem and outlining our objectives. Then I briefly described all the options we have considered, one of which was to do nothing. Then I outlined our proposed course of action to solve the problem—which of course was to purchase new equipment—and briefly explained how we intended to overcome some of the potential problems we might encounter. Headquarters approved the proposal in six days instead of the usual six months. And there was no battle to be fought!"

Once people agree there is a problem, they cross an important psychological threshold. By agreeing that there is a problem, they also must *almost simultaneously* agree that we need a solution. It's hard for me to imagine anyone agreeing there is a problem and not agreeing that it must be solved. Therefore, to propose a solution without first agreeing that there is a problem is almost frivolous. Yet people do it all the time.

Time and again I see people fall into Geoffrey's old trap. They propose a solution without getting clear consensus that there is a problem. The result is the person making the proposal is immediately placed on the defensive by having to prove that there actually is a problem to be solved or a benefit to be achieved by agreeing to the course of action proposed.

Don't take the shortcut by jumping to the proposed course of action first. It almost always turns out to be the long cut in the long run. Frame your proposals by outlining the problem and your stated objectives first.

21

Double Your Brain Power

Your subconscious mind works differently than your conscious mind in many ways. Your subconscious mind is the part of your mind that likes things to be complete, finished, and whole. Your conscious mind often doesn't care if things are left unfinished or incomplete. Your subconscious mind doesn't like unsolved problems. Your conscious mind could care less if some problems are left unsolved. In fact, your subconscious mind will often put barriers in your way that prevent you from reaching conclusions.

Writers often experience a phenomena they call "writer's block." They just can't think of things to write, or maybe they have an idea but can't come up with a way to express the idea effectively in words. Trying harder simply leads to greater frustration. Many writers say, however, that if they let go of it—stop trying to force a solution—and engage in some other activity for a while, then later on when they sit down to try again, the words flow easily.

The explanation for this phenomenon is simple. Often when we force a problem on our conscious minds, it resists. It digs its heels in and prevents us from finding a solution. When we let go of the problem or challenge with our conscious mind, our subconscious mind, which doesn't like unfinished business or unsolved problems, takes over and works the problem on its own until a viable solution is reached.

This is exactly what happens when you can picture someone's face but can't think of the person's name. The harder you try, the more frustrated you become. So you stop trying and move on to another task. Then sometime later, aha! The name occurs to you, seemingly out of the blue.

Guess what? It didn't come out of the blue. While you were consciously focusing on other activities, your subconscious mind continued to sort through all the faces in your memory banks, comparing each to all the names you had stored, until it came up with a match. Then when bridging occurred between your conscious and subconscious mind, your subconscious mind kicked the name up to your conscious mind, creating the impression that the name came out of nowhere when it actually came from your subconscious. The reason why these tidbits often surface when you're driving, doing housework, showering, getting dressed in the morning, or carrying out other routine activities is that a great deal of bridging back and forth between conscious and subconscious thought processes takes place during these routine activities.

Another example is when you lose something—like your car keys. The harder you look, the more difficult it is and the more frustrated you become. Stop looking for a while, stop thinking about the keys, and do something else. Again, seemingly out of the blue, you remember where you put them.

The location of the keys didn't come out of nowhere. Your subconscious mind, which likes everything in its proper place, can't stand it that something is lost. So your subconscious mind will—on its own—retrace your steps and inventory your activities until it remembers where you put the keys. Then when a bridging opportunity arises, it kicks the information up to your conscious level of awareness.

By the way, this is one reason you should never set a goal to *lose* weight. Show me someone who has "lost weight" and I'll show you someone whose subconscious mind will find that weight and put it right back where it belongs—every time.

Rather than "lose weight," either whet your goal to weigh the amount you want to weigh or set a goal to permanently get rid of a certain number of pounds. The best way is to visualize yourself weighing the amount you want to weigh; then your subconscious mind will work on your behalf to help get rid of the weight that doesn't belong.

A successful dieter may not realize it, but when he or she truly is committed to getting rid of weight for good—no matter what weight-loss method is chosen—you can bet that this person has a clear mental image of the dress she will be wearing soon or the way he'll feel when he runs a 5K or plays tennis with his daughter. More than that, a successful weight loser has a clear image of the desired weight or pound loss. This clear, conscious goal enables the dieter to embark on a new way of eating and exercising without getting bogged down by the temptations and obstacles along the way. But this is just one application of the principle.

The best way to double your brain power is to recognize when your conscious mind has reached its limits or is blocking your problem-solving process. Then take a break and turn over your problem-solving efforts to your subconscious mind for a reasonable period of time. Sometimes this might be overnight or even a day or two. Then when you come back to the task, whether it's writing something important or solving a complex problem, you're likely to either have the solution or, at the very least, have a better sense of how to proceed toward a better solution.

When you do this, keep a pad of paper and pencil next to your bed. Or you might even keep a small tape recorder handy. Sometimes you'll wake up in the middle of the night with an idea or an answer that you'll want to capture to carry forward into your work the next day.

22

Only Your *Name Goes on Your Resumé*

Don't use a bad boss as an excuse for bad performance. We've all had them. And the more bosses we've had, the more bad ones we've likely endured. So next year when you're looking for a job, don't plan on saying, "The reason I didn't perform well last year was because I worked for <u>insert name of bad boss.</u>"

Nobody cares who your boss was. The interviewer, or prospective new boss, might start thinking, "What if you think I'm a bad boss, too. Maybe I'd better not risk it."

It's much better to be a top performer anyway—in spite of your bad boss. It's much better to be a top performer than to let a new prospective boss, or even a colleague, know how bad your boss was (see Chapter 1—"Everyone Knows"). They'll see you not only as a top performer who doesn't make excuses (see Chapter 18—"Excuses Will Kill You"), but they'll also see you as someone who can *overcome adversity*. This is not a bad label to carry around.

So the next time you're thinking about cutting corners or slacking off from your own personal high standards out of resentment for your boss, co-workers, somebody in another department, or whomever, DON'T DO IT! Maintain your standards no matter what so you can demonstrate a consistent track record of achievement.

23

Get Help When You Need It

I never cease to be amazed at the number of people I encounter who face a challenge, obstacle, or problem and refuse to get help. The reasons people don't seek help abound. For some people it's because they don't want to feel weak or inferior ("If I ask you for help, I'm not so strong as you."). For others it's because they don't want to impose on someone else's good graces. Others have been conditioned that you "take care of yourself, no matter what." Still others don't ask for help because they lack trust—they believe other people will take advantage of them if they appear vulnerable. And the list could go on.

If there's one lesson we've learned from the life experiences of all those who have preceded us, however, it's that life is tough and that at various times in our lives each of us will face problems that we'll need help solving.

Time and again, studies have shown that the people who are most successful in life are also people who are most effective in: 1) understanding when they need help, 2) asking for help when they need it, and 3) going to the right people to get the right kind of help when they ask for it.

If you don't encounter real world obstacles and significant challenges that stand in the way of achieving your goals, then you aren't setting goals that are high enough. When you encounter challenges, you should accept the challenges as feedback that you are on your way toward something significant.

This is true, by the way, for parenting and having a happy and fulfilling marriage too. Of course there will be challenges. The challenges exist because the rewards are so great. Respond to the challenges by getting the right help, not by avoiding the challenges, pretending they don't exist, or blaming the circumstances on things you can't influence.

Everyone encounters problems. Successful people in any arena or any endeavor respond to the most significant of those challenges by seeking out the right kind of help. The operant phrase here is "the right kind" of help.

My wife and I made a pact early in our marriage that when either of us needed help, we would commit to giving the help we thought was *needed* rather than the help that might be *wanted* in different situations. This agreement has made our marriage strong and helped us to be stronger individually as well.

It's important that the people to whom we go for help give us the help that we truly need rather than the help we imagine we need. Sometimes we are able to recognize objectively the kind of help we need. But many other times we aren't so objective. We can imagine (or desire) one kind of help to solve our perceived problem when, in truth, we need different help that isn't so pleasant to receive. A simple example would be how I might get help in satisfying my mid-afternoon hunger. I might go to my wife and say, "I'm hungry, let's have a bowl of ice cream." My problem is my hunger and my way of solving it is to eat a bowl of ice cream. However, she realizes I should be watching my diet so she says, "Have an apple instead." The response I *want* is to share a bowl of ice cream. The answer that's more appropriate or *needed,* all things considered, is to have an apple.

Perhaps you've seen the consummate English chef and successful restaurateur Gordon Ramsey as he devotes two weeks (condensed into a 30-minute television show) running around a failing restaurant. How often are the failing restaurant owners blinded—even obstinately resistant—to their own needs? Their spouse, employees, and customers know what's truly needed. But the person wants a different, less painful "help." In a sense it goes back to problem solving: The failing restaurateur does not, or is not willing, to acknowledge the true problem. Of course in the show Ramsey eventually sets them straight and things turn around. It's easy to watch someone else's "deer in headlights" reaction to true help. And it's an easy image to keep in mind when we need to seek true help.

I can't count the number of times I've seen people ask for help from people who will tell them what they *want* to hear rather than what they *need* to hear. I recall a more significant example that occurred when I was an area developer for a national franchisor. A woman bought a franchise from our company and went into business for herself. She'd never been in business for herself before, so a franchise seemed like a good move. After all, she could capitalize on all the expertise, business programs, and marketing savvy of the franchisor. But she created problems for herself from the outset because she wouldn't listen to the franchisor's advice. She was convinced she knew better. Time and again I would meet with her or she'd talk to someone from the franchise company, and we'd give her tested and proven advice. She'd convince herself that her way was better. But even worse, she'd then turn to a few other people, including her husband, for "help" to get their input about what they thought she should do. She'd present her dilemma in a way that made her preferences clear. Unfortunately for her, they'd all pick up on her cues and encourage her to do it her way. When her way didn't work, they'd gather around her and find ways to help her conclude it was the franchisor's fault.

This was one of the saddest cases I've ever seen, because everyone's intentions were noble, even though their actions were destructive. The franchisee felt like she had a loyal and trustworthy inner circle of advisors. The advisors felt like they were providing crucial support. But because the support they provided wasn't based on the help she most needed, this lady's trusted helpers unwittingly led her to failure and bankruptcy.

The moral of the story: Get help when you need it … but make sure it's the help you *need*, regardless of what you may feel you want.

24

Be a Helper

My brother, Rob, is a talented and successful businessman, realtor, and real estate developer in Scottsdale, Arizona. He established a reputation early in his career as a top-notch troubleshooter and problem solver in his field. Because of his reputation an investor came to him for a solution to his problem. The investor had talked to numerous other people and was dissatisfied with the advice each had given him up to that point. After listening to the investor's dilemma, Rob devised a way for the investor to solve his problem and outlined the plan to the investor. The investor reviewed the plan and responded that it made sense, but he couldn't figure out why Rob was helping him. What was in Rob's plan for Rob? Rob replied truthfully that he would receive no personal benefit from his proposal, but that his plan was the best way out for the investor; therefore, that's what he should do.

The investor walked away in amazement and proceeded to solve his problem by following Rob's advice.

As you might have already guessed, the story didn't end there. The investor was so impressed that he came back to Rob with another deal that allowed Rob to earn a great deal of money (along with the investor). Based on the trust and mutual respect they developed, this led to other deals and an ongoing relationship worth well into eight or nine figures.

The moral of the story:

Give help when it's needed if you're in a position to help.

Do that and the rewards will follow. Don't always screen every request for help by asking, "What's in it for me?"

I encounter similar kinds of situations all the time as a consultant who helps people with their businesses and their careers. People ask for advice, and I give the best I can give. I'll admit that sometimes the problem they're trying to solve, especially if it's a business problem, is so challenging and complex that my recommendation is that they hire me to help solve it. But in these cases I'm only being honest about what it will take to meet their needs. If, however, I can answer the question and help them up front, I will. It's nice to see, then, how many of these people turn to me first when later on they encounter a bigger challenge.

In both examples above it might sound like the reason you should help others is because in the long run you'll be rewarded nicely for doing so. Yes, most of the time you will, and most of the time the rewards will come in unexpected ways that exceed your expectations. But that's not the real reason to help others when they need it.

Help others when they need it because it's the right thing to do. Using your natural gifts and talents to benefit others is one reason you have been given those talents. Life is tough for everyone. We all need help from time to time in order to overcome the challenges we each face. Be one of the helpers and don't expect anything in return. Then when your time comes, maybe it will be easier for you to ask for the help you need.

25

Use Your Resumé to Manage Your Career

One of the easiest ways to set career-related goals is to review your resumé with a critical eye at least once a year. I usually pick the week just prior to New Year's Day each year.

Ask yourself the following questions:

1. Is my career, as reflected in my resumé, progressing the way I want it to? If so, what do I need to build on to keep the momentum going? If not, what changes should I make?
2. What contribution-oriented achievements (see Chapter 2—"The Most Important Question You Can Ask") can I pursue during the upcoming year that will make me more valuable to current or future employers?
3. What development activities can I pursue that will demonstrate on my resumé that I am growing and becoming more knowledgeable and, therefore, more valuable in my field?

Then set goals—two or three per quarter—to enhance your marketability in your field. Some of your goals might be to attend different workshops, seminars, or training programs. Some could be to acquire new skills. Others could be to work on certain kinds of projects.

You might even set larger goals, such as changing jobs or changing careers. (If your goal is to change careers, I recommend you first read

What Color is Your Parachute?[7] by Richard Nelson Bolles. It's the best-selling manual of all time for career changers.)

If you want to be more rigorous in your approach, show your resume to two or three people you respect and who can offer valid advice. Then ask them the same questions listed above before finalizing your list of goals for the year. Peruse one of Jack Canfield's latest books entitled *The Success Principles*[8] to help stimulate your thinking even more on the things you can be doing to provide yourself a greater degree of success.

Be consistent in conducting this assessment and goal-setting process year after year and your career will be built upon a foundation of success that no one can ever take away from you.

---

[7] Richard Nelson Bolles, *What Color is Your Parachute?* (Berkeley, CA: Ten Speed Press, 2009).

[8] Jack Canfield, *The Success Principles: How to Get from Where You Are to Where You Want to Be* (New York: HarperCollins, 2005).

26

Achieve Communication Supremacy

When two people communicate, the process looks like this:

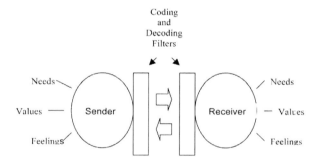

Figure 26.1 Elements of Interpersonal Communication

The sender develops an impulse to send a message in response to specific needs, values, or feelings. In order to transmit the message the sender must "code" the message by committing it to words, language, and perhaps nonverbal messages. The words, language, and nonverbal messages which the sender uses will be determined based on a set of filters unique to the sender that have been developed as a result of the sender's training and life experiences.

The receiver then must "de-code" the message through a different filter that is unique to the receiver and influenced by the receiver's current needs, values, and feelings.

Because the coding and de-coding processes are complex and based on filters unique to each person, there can be no such thing as effective one-way communication over the long haul. In order to ensure effectiveness, communication must be two way. In other words, there needs to be feedback from the receiver to the sender that confirms understanding of the transmitted message.

The biggest mistake many people make when communicating is to accept responsibility *only* for their side of the equation. How many times have you heard someone say, "I told them what to do. They just don't get it"? Or, even worse, how many times have you heard, "I told them a million times, and they still don't get it"? Implied in this statement is the thought, "They must really be dumb if I've told them so many times and they still don't get it."

But the reality is: Communication is about what others hear, not about what you say.

Ask yourself this: Who's the dumb one here if the sender keeps sending the same message over and over with the same result, namely, that the receiver doesn't get it? The sender has a responsibility to change the way the message is sent if it's not understood the first time (and the second time, and the third time, and so on) until it is understood. Show me someone who blames the other person if that person doesn't get something after numerous communication attempts, and I'll show you a poor communicator.

Sometimes senders must accept responsibility for both sides of the communication process. As a sender, I must not only strive to be a good sender, but I must also strive to help the listener to be a good listener. As a receiver, there will be plenty of times when I not only have to be a good listener, but I must also strive to help the sender to be a good sender.

Don't put someone down or, even worse, accept mediocre results because someone else isn't either a good sender or a good receiver. Rise to the occasion and make sure that all your communications are effective, regardless of the skill level of the other person.

Have you ever wondered what separates the really outstanding communicators from the rest? The key trait that separates the super communicators from the average and poor ones is that the super communicators accept responsibility for the total process, for both sender and receiver. Super communicators make sure that the needs, values, and feelings on both sides are satisfied—not just their own.

Blaming someone else for a communication breakdown brings little satisfaction if the reality is that a communication breakdown occurred. Communicate in such a way that communication breakdown is avoided and you'll never have to worry about who to blame.

27

Avoid the Writing Trap

Since the advent of email, we've heard many people sing its praises. We've also heard a few criticisms. But the one criticism that very few people talk about is how many people have pooped on the porch by saying things in emails that they shouldn't have.

I'm sure the percentage of people getting in trouble over things they say in emails is not much higher than the percentage of people who have created trouble for themselves with more formal written correspondence such as memos, letters, and reports. But because the number of emails most people send is so much higher than the number of other written correspondence, the number of people getting in trouble and the actual number of incidents have soared.

Rules to remember when you put something in writing.

1. Assume it will someday be seen by everyone.
2. Sarcasm often backfires—don't be sarcastic or cynical unless you're absolutely certain you can't be misunderstood.
3. The standards of politically correctness are higher for the written than for the spoken word. If there's any possibility that what you write could be seen as politically incorrect, don't write it.
4. Written statements can be quoted out of context. Don't write things that only can be interpreted the way you intend

if they are read and digested in full context of everything else you've written.
5. Use short, simple, easy-to-understand sentences to minimize the opportunity for misunderstanding.

Questions to keep in mind when sending written messages.

1. Would this embarrass me if certain people see it? If the answer is yes or maybe, don't put it in writing.
2. Would this embarrass anyone else if certain people see it? If the answer is yes or maybe, don't put it in writing.
3. Am I proud of what I've written? In other words, do these words project an image of me that I want others to see when they think of me?
4. Does everything I've written represent me as a competent, caring, and responsible person?

Remember, everything you write is a representation of you in your absence. It is *always* in your best interest to ensure that everything "on the street" that is tied to you represents you in the best possible manner (see Chapter 4—"Why Worry about Perceptions?").

28

Leadership Makes a Difference

The one area where we have made the greatest gains in understanding relative to human and organizational performance during the past century is the area of leadership. In fact, the greatest gains in actual bottom-line performance have resulted from improvements in both our understanding of leadership and our ability to apply this knowledge productively.

Today it's understood that leadership is practiced in one of five different contexts:

1. Leading self
2. Leading others in one-to-one relationships
3. Leading small groups or teams
4. Leading organizations
5. Leading strategic alliances that are created between organizations

Everyone with a job or a career today would perform better in all areas of their lives if they each became a masterful self leader. "Self leader" means taking charge of our own development and performance in support of whatever teams to which we belong and in terms of the organization for which we work. Ultimate career success depends upon our ability to lead ourselves successfully to fulfillment of both individual and corporate goals.

Additionally, everyone with a job or a career today would perform better if they possessed at least a minimum level of team leadership expertise. Whether or not we're ever specifically made a team *leader*, we will all likely be team *members* frequently during our careers. The more we know about effective teamwork and team leadership, the better a team member we'll be. Regardless of our technical expertise or ability, it is important to also possess certain process skills—especially in the area of team processes—so that we can help create the synergies desired through team effort (see Chapter 2—"The Secret to Leveraging Your Performance").

Once you've established yourself as an effective team player, the next level of leadership you'll want to learn is how to lead others in a one-to-one context. This will require that you be an effective coach and mentor as well as being able to energize followers to maximize their performances.

Organizational leadership is a bit more complex and centers mostly on having the ability to implement initiatives that will lead the organization to sustained excellence. Typical skills required of leaders in the organizational context include scanning the environment, organizational visioning and goal setting, framing initiatives properly, and managing change.

Leading strategic alliances is the newest area of organizational leadership, which was developed over the past couple of decades. Alliances are formal relationships that exist between two organizations to leverage their individual resources in order to achieve some bigger, mutually beneficial, long-term purpose.

Taken together, the five leadership contexts (Leading Self, Leading One to One, Leading Teams, Leading Organizations, Leading Alliances) form the basis for the term "Leadership in Context." This understanding represents the future in regard to organizational leadership theory and practice. But don't worry about this too much at this point. We will delve deeper into understanding Leadership in Context later in Chapter 35, "Be Effectively Flexible." Much greater depth about the SOTOA Model can be found in the book *ACHIEVE LEADERSHIP GENIUS: How You Lead Depends on Who, What, Where, and When You Lead*, by Drea Zigarmi, Susan Fowler, and Dick Lyles, iUniverse, 2010.

29

Don't Let Others Be Responsible for Your Success

To the degree you rely on others for your success, you will be correspondingly disappointed. Get their input. Ask for help when needed. But don't pin the hopes of your ultimate success on their performance.

How many times have you heard someone say they didn't achieve their objective—maybe they missed a deadline, failed to ship something on time, or didn't complete a project on schedule—because someone else didn't get them something they needed when they needed it? It happens all the time. "I couldn't do my job because so-and-so didn't do his!"

When you allow this to happen to you, you'll get burned every time. And you'll pay the price, because it's *your* objective that wasn't met, and *your* responsibilities that went unfilled. It's not okay to say, "The reason I didn't deliver is because of so-and-so" (see Chapter 22—"Only *Your* Name Goes on Your Resumé").

The situation is different if you're a leader counting on your followers (see Chapter 28—"Leadership Makes a Difference"). When you are the leader, you're definitely pinning your hopes on your abilities as a leader to get your followers to deliver. You *are* responsible for their performance, which is different. In this case you must accept the responsibility for their performance.

But in the absence of formal authority, you must be more strategic. If input from others is required for your success, *it is up to you* to see to it that appropriate input is received in a timely fashion *so that your objectives are met*. No one else cares enough about *your* objectives (except maybe your boss) to be relied upon to get you what you need when you need it.

Therefore, it is important for you to plan, negotiate, nudge, badger, nag, plead, beg, work around, develop alternate strategies, threaten, cajole, pray, entice, bribe, manipulate, coerce, or do anything else that might be necessary *and effective* in seeing to it that your objectives are met. This might seem counterintuitive, so let me give you an example.

I once consulted with a company that was in a very intense growth mode. Because of the rapid growth, the Human Resources department was swamped with staffing and hiring requests and was understaffed. All the managers in the company complained about how their results were suffering because they couldn't bring on enough good people fast enough. All but one. The only person who never complained was Barney, the manufacturing manager. He didn't complain because he didn't need to. He had the same recruiting demands as everyone else, but his needs were always met.

One day I asked Barney how he was able to keep fully staffed while everyone else remained way behind the power curve. "Easy," he replied. "Everyone else thinks hiring is a *paper* process. They fill out their staffing request forms and submit them along with all the others. I see it as a *people* process. Every Monday morning after the Human Resources director has had a chance to settle in, I pop in and visit her. I bring all my new paperwork and review the status of previous requests. I ask what has been done to fill my vacancies and what the plans are for this week. Because she knows I'll be there every Monday, she makes sure she has both progress to report and plans to discuss. My work always holds top-of-mind awareness for her."

Sounds simple, doesn't it? Why don't more people do it? Maybe because they think it's easier to blame Human Resources for their shortcomings than to go to the trouble of ensuring there are no shortcomings. Remember, though, you can't send out your resumé with an asterisk that says, "My performance was lousy that year because HR didn't get me the people I needed."

The same is true for every other person or group you need for success. Your success is in your hands. It's up to you to get from them what you need to be successful.

30

The Hidden Power of Mentors

Ronald Reagan had a "kitchen cabinet" both as Governor of the State of California and during his term as President of the United States. Renowned motivational speaker and author Napoleon Hill encouraged everyone to have a mastermind group. Whether you call it a kitchen cabinet, a mastermind group, or simply just your own inner circle of trusted confidants and advisors, you should have one.

Who are your mentors? Who do you turn to for technical or specialized knowledge in areas pertinent to your career or business? Who is your spiritual advisor? From whom do you seek input when making significant career decisions? Do you have someone to whom you turn for help with financial matters? What about real estate matters?

You need to have several people on whom you can rely to give you trustworthy advice and guidance, to help you through your life and your career. If you don't have these mentors, you need to find some.

Life is too complex and the challenges we face too daunting for us to presume that we can face them all by ourselves (see Chapter 23—"Get Help When You Need It"). When you exclude others from the process, you are certain to leave opportunity on the table, so to speak, and at the very least make decisions that are not always optimal.

Your mentors need to be a group of people rather than one person. It's unlikely that you'll turn to the mechanic who services your car for spiritual advice, and even more unlikely that you'll go to your pastor for guidance on the investment decisions you make in your business.

So what's needed is a diverse group of people, each with their own area of knowledge and expertise. But it's not a group of people who will necessarily know each other. In fact, they may probably never even meet each other. It's a group of individuals with whom you have special relationships that allow you to call them on the phone or take them to lunch and pick their brains.

Areas of expertise in which you might identify someone specific to be your mentor might include spirituality, career, technical areas, finance, real estate, medical, and legal. More often than not you'll use these mentors to give you advice regarding decisions you are about to make. Sometimes their advice will be in the form of a second opinion, and sometimes they'll play the role of educator, helping you to more fully understand the situation confronting you.

The most important trait of your mentors, though, is that they must tell you what you *need* to hear as opposed to what you *want* to hear when you ask for advice. People who simply say "yes" to everything you propose and encourage you forward no matter what you do are not good mentors. In fact, they create a recipe for disaster by giving you false confidence as you're heading for failure. So pick your mentors wisely. And don't be surprised if you need different mentors as you grow in expertise and understanding along the way.

31

USE YOUR SELF TALK TO YOUR ADVANTAGE

Let's begin with a simple, indisputable fact: *Your image of yourself regulates your behavior over time.* In other words, more than anything else, who you think you are will determine how you will act. There is truth to the age-old axiom, "As I think, I am."

How many people have you seen (or maybe you are one of those people) who are perfectly good communicators in one-on-one situations yet *think* they can't speak effectively to larger groups? The basic skills of articulation and verbalization are the same in both situations, so it isn't a question of ability. But because the person *thinks* they aren't so effective in the large group, they don't perform as well in a large group.

Another good example can be presented using the game of golf. Most golfers have an image, oftentimes based on past performance, of their performance ability as a golfer. Once established, that image will go a long way to regulate a golfer's ongoing performance. If the golfer is playing worse than usual on a given day, there's a very good chance the golfer will have a few better-than-normal shots toward the end of the day. ("See, I knew I wasn't that bad.") Along the same line, if a golfer is having an exceptionally good day—playing well above his or her usual—then it's a pretty safe bet that the last few holes won't be played as well. ("It never fails. That's just the way I play!")

The only way to sustain changes in your behavior is to first change your image. When your mind envisions an image of yourself that it believes to be valid, that image will drive your behavior over time.

Behavior conforms to image. When the two are out of alignment (for example, when your golf performance is better or worse than your image), then tension will grow in your subconscious mind until alignment is restored. The greater the difference between your image and your behavior, the greater will be the tension to eliminate the difference. Unless you change your image—a choice most people avoid—you can't hope to sustain changes in your behavior.

Another way to picture this dynamic is to imagine a set of scales with your self image on one side and your behavior on the other, as shown in Figure 31.1.

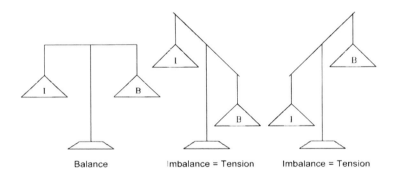

Figure 31.1 Tension When Behavior is Out of Balance with Image

If an imbalance occurs between your image of yourself and your behavior, the imbalance will create tension until balance is restored. The direction of the imbalance doesn't matter, but the magnitude does. The greater the discrepancy between your image and your behavior, the greater the tension you will experience until balance is restored.

The tension people experience when there is a discrepancy between their behavior and their image often leads to even more overt emotions, such as embarrassment. An example of this could be the person who is not a heavy drinker, but goes to a party, drinks too much, gets drunk, and acts foolishly. The next day they remember (or find out from others) what happened and become extremely embarrassed. Unless they're an alcoholic (which is a different problem), that embarrassment, and all the other tension that is created along with the behavioral discrepancy, will cause the person to act more normally at the next party. In fact, the person might avoid drinking altogether at the next opportunity just to prove "I'm not that way."

If the regulator of our behavior is our self image, then how do we change our image?

We change our image through our self talk. Self talk is how we talk to ourselves about ourselves, something we do all the time, often without realizing it. What we say about ourselves shapes the way we think about ourselves. All the little messages we send have a cumulative effect in shaping our self images. How we react to our behavior, how we react to the things other people say about us, and simply how we describe ourselves all have the effect over time of shaping our image of ourselves.

Figure 31.2 shows how this all comes together in a logical way. Our self image drives our behavior. We respond to our behavior or to things we've heard from other people with self talk which, in turn, shapes our self image.

Logic tells us that the best way to change our behavior is to change our image. If we change our behavior without changing our image, the change won't last, because tension will be created that will cause the behavior to re-align with our image. The way to change the image is by programming our self talk.

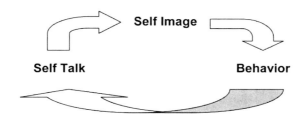

Figure 31.2 How Self Talk and Self Image Shape Personal Behavior

The key to achieving any change in performance or behavior is to make relevant and appropriate changes in your self talk. Here's how it works:

1. Decide what changes you want to make.

2. Make statements about yourself in positive, present-tense language as if the changes have already been achieved.
3. Repeat those statements regularly *and* make sure that positive assumptions are reflected in all other statements you make about yourself.

Consider an example from my own experience. Years ago when I was in college I started smoking. I quickly became a regular smoker, smoking at least half a pack a day. I took the habit with me into the Navy after I was commissioned as a Naval Officer. After a few years I decided to try to quit. Every time I tried to quit, I changed my behavior without changing either my self talk or, most importantly, my self image.

When people would offer me a cigarette I'd say, "No thanks. I'm trying to quit." Think about what this message tells me about myself. It says, "I'm a smoker who's trying to quit." If my image is that I'm a smoker trying to quit, then how must I act in order to eliminate any tension between my behavior and my image? I must first smoke; otherwise, I can't try to quit. Next I must *try* to quit without actually quitting, because once I quit, I can no longer try.

If I want to quit smoking, then what's the key? The key is to talk about myself—to myself—as though I'm already a nonsmoker. So if someone offers me a cigarette, my answer should be, "No, thanks. I don't smoke." Every time I say this about myself, I reinforce my image of myself as a nonsmoker. Eventually, it becomes harder for me to smoke, because I believe and think about myself as a nonsmoker, rather than as a smoker who's trying to quit.

The same thing happens to people who try to lose weight or who try to do anything, for that matter. People who try, try; people who do, do.

So how do you make this work for you?

- First set goals for yourself. (Weigh a vibrant 120 or 185 pounds—or whatever is a realistic, healthy weight for you.)
- Translate each goal into a positive, present-tense statement as if it were already achieved. (I weigh 160 pounds and look and feel great.) It's okay to have more than one such

statement. (I eat only the healthy foods I need to maintain my weight at 160 pounds. I exercise regularly to keep my weight at 160 pounds.)
- Write these positive, present-tense statements on cards that you carry with you and READ AND REPEAT THEM WHENEVER POSSIBLE. Each time you repeat them, you will be programming your self image to create tension that will pull your behavior in the right direction.
- Make sure that in all your other conversations when you refer to yourself, you refer to yourself AS IF THESE STATEMENTS WERE TRUE. (For example, "No, thanks, I don't smoke," even though the smoker may still be in the throes of quitting.)
- Ensure that you filter the things other people say about you through the filter of your positive, present-tense statements. If someone says or implies something about you that is contrary to your statements, you should rebut it *in your own mind*. There's no need to get into a big argument with the person about what's true and what isn't. Simply say to yourself, "That's not me. Even though that person's perception may be real to them, it's not valid as far as I'm concerned. THIS is who I am."
- Revisit your goals and statements regularly to ensure they are aligned. Rewrite different statements if needed to freshen them and add vitality on a regular basis.

Perhaps the most important thing to remember regarding self talk is that you should audit yourself on a regular basis to make sure that the things you say *and imply* about yourself reinforce the image of the person you want to be. "As I think, I am," is a fundamental truism. The way you control how you think about yourself is to control how you talk about yourself.

32

Feedback Is the Breakfast of Champions

Assume for a moment you are a supervisor who hires two people to work for you: Jennifer and Jason. Further assume that both have pretty much the same qualifications, experience, skill set, and knowledge when they come aboard. You give them each assignments that are similar in scope and requirements. Let's say the assignments take a week to complete, and they are submitted to you with about an equal number of discrepancies, understandable because of the level of performance each is capable of achieving.

You approach Jason and advise him of all the discrepancies and ask him to correct them. But you're hesitant to do the same with Jennifer. Perhaps you're concerned about how she might react or that she might think you're picking on her for some reason. Regardless of the reason, you decide not to give her the same feedback.

Assume even further that this pattern goes on for a year. Every time you notice discrepancies in Jason's performance, you correct them; every time you notice discrepancies in Jennifer's performance, you either correct them yourself or ignore them.

At the end of a year you leave your position. Your boss wants to promote someone to fill your vacancy and must choose between Jennifer and Jason. Based on the scenario just described, which one will be the most qualified?

Jason will be the most qualified because on an ongoing basis he received the developmental feedback necessary for him to learn, grow, and become better at his job.

Jennifer won't be as qualified because you cheated her out of the opportunity to learn and develop by withholding that same beneficial feedback. Is this fair? No. In fact, the law calls this practice "covert discrimination." You will have unfairly discriminated against Jennifer by denying her the same opportunity to develop that you gave Jason. Simply stated, you cheated her.

Feedback is necessary for growth. If you want others to succeed, give them the feedback they need to develop or correct their behavior as necessary to progress through their careers. If you want to succeed, make sure you're getting the feedback you need in order to develop or correct your own behavior in ways that will lead to success.

No one can get all the information they need about their performance and their impact on others without feedback. To the extent that you miss out on this important data, you are being cheated out of the opportunity to achieve your fullest possible potential. To the extent that you receive this important information, you will become a champion in your field.

Feedback is, indeed, the breakfast of champions. Make sure you get yours.

33

The Most Important Virtue

Winston Churchill said it during World War II; Rudy Giuliani said it in the wake of 9/11:

> ***Courage is the most important virtue because without it, all others will fail.***

34

Master the Effectiveness Equation

Sometimes life isn't fair. One of those times is when people work hard to find the right answer—a true, high-quality solution to a particular problem—and their solution gets blown out of the water.

It's a rude introduction to the reality that when dealing with solutions to problems or the effective implementation of a decision, having the right answer is not enough. In addition to having a high-quality solution, it is also necessary to gain acceptance for that solution, either by the people above you in the organization who must approve the idea or by the people elsewhere in the organization who will implement it. Your overall effectiveness will depend almost equally on both. You must have a quality idea *and* you must gain acceptance for the idea from the necessary people. This principle can best be stated through the use of a mathematical equation as follows:

$$\text{Effectiveness} = f(\text{Quality} \times \text{Acceptance})$$
$$\text{Effectiveness} = f(Q \times A)$$

If you play around with this equation by substituting numerical values for Q and for A, you quickly find that the way to optimize effectiveness is to maximize both quality and acceptance. Lowering the value of either will automatically lower effectiveness.

This equation provided the basis for the argument in favor of "participative management" back in the '70s. Many theorists argued that participation in problem solving and decision making leads to ownership of the outcome. And since ownership of a solution or decision is the highest form of acceptance, the best way to maximize the equation is to maximize involvement or ownership of participants. This led to disaster in many circumstances because it assumed universal competence, which would also maximize the quality side of the equation—and this assumption was wrong. Many people who were invited to participate weren't qualified—either with the right skills, the right knowledge, or both—so the results were strong ownership of some pretty lousy solutions. Instead of capitalizing on our resources, we were pooling our ignorance.

Bombing out on either side of the equation leads to trouble, as this equation shows:

$$\text{Effectiveness} = f(100 \times 0) = 0$$
$$\text{Effectiveness} = f(0 \times 100) = 0$$

How do we master the effectiveness equation?

The answer depends on the circumstance. In some cases you might choose the right people to get involved in the decision-making process. These people will bring both the necessary expertise and the authority to implement the decision effectively. In other cases, however, you will have the person or people with the right expertise solve the problem or arrive at the necessary decision. This maximizes quality. Then you maximize effectiveness by selling the decision to those people who either must approve it or implement it. It isn't enough to get the right answer to a solution; you must also achieve the right results. That is to say, the right answer must be implemented.

This is the reason my problem-solving process consists of seven steps rather than four (see Chapter 14—"How to Be a Problem-Solving Super Star"). The first four steps involve getting the right answer while all seven steps, and particularly the last three, focus on achieving the right result. It's not an accident that step five focuses on troubleshooting and step six focuses on communicating to gain acceptance of (or to sell) your proposed action plan before implementing it in step seven.

Whether you "solve then sell" or "sell while solving," the more you recognize the need to both solve and sell in order to get results, the more effective you'll be.

35

Be Effectively Flexible

Back in the days of door-to-door encyclopedia sales, the publishers trained salespeople with one basic technique that was scripted in great detail. If a salesperson were good with this technique, he could count on selling a set of encyclopedias to two out of every thirty prospects. Salespeople were told to knock on fifty doors a day. If they knocked on fifty doors a day, in those days they would meet on average thirty people. Out of those thirty people, the salesmen would average two sales.

Modern day telemarketers work the same way. With a given script the company knows that the telemarketer will succeed with a small percentage of people. So the strategy is to call as many people as possible, knowing that the salesperson and the company will make money on the small percentage of successful calls.

The question to ask is what about all the people who didn't buy in response to the pitch? Does this mean they weren't in the market for encyclopedias or whatever else the direct marketers had to offer? No. It only means that they didn't respond to this particular pitch.

Would another pitch perhaps produce a different result? Probably. Having more pitches could yield increased sales substantially. But the problem is that it's too hard to teach several pitches to salespeople, and it's even more difficult to teach salespeople when it's time to shift gears and use a different approach. Instead it's easier just to train people in one way and make the whole process a numbers game—from the company's perspective.

But you are, and must be, much more nimble than a one-pitch sales operation in order to be effective. This is true whether talking about sales or any other endeavor. It's critical for your personal effectiveness to learn different approaches toward influencing people and to be flexible and adaptable in using different styles effectively. Otherwise, you'll miss out on an abundance of opportunities that you really shouldn't have to pass up.

In fact, there are at least three areas in which it is critical to commit to lifelong learning and developing your adaptability. These three areas are: your inner, spiritual life; your interpersonal behavior, and your leadership skills. For the purposes of this book we'll deal only with the latter two. In both of these areas, the more flexible you can be in responding to the different personalities you encounter, the more successful you will be.

To illustrate what I mean by "flexibility," let's examine just one behavior, namely, the way that individuals give and receive information. Clearly there is a vast range—a continuum—of different ways in which individuals prefer to give and receive information. At one end of the continuum are people who are very direct—people who are succinct and to the point and who like to "tell it like it is" without "beating around the bush." At the other end of the continuum are people who are quite indirect—people who like to lead up to their key points gradually and who often hint at, or infer, the points they most want to convey. Logic tells us that if I'm brutally direct with someone who prefers indirectness, then I'm more likely to put him off than to elicit my desired response. I'm equally likely to cause a negative reaction if I'm indirect with someone who prefers directness. In this latter case, the person who prefers information delivered directly and to the point might wrongly perceive my indirect approach as evasive, misleading, or manipulative. There are numerous continuums like this that describe individual behavioral and processing preferences and tendencies.

The framework tool that I've found most valuable to evaluate other people's processing preferences is the DISC Model because it lends itself to immediate and practical application. (For more information you can search the Internet for DISC Model.) There are several other framework tools you might consider. What's most important is that you seek out ways to understand your own behavioral preferences and how to either parallel or collide with the behavioral preferences of other people.

The second area of flexibility or adaptability that we'll cover here is in the area of leadership. A mistaken approach toward leadership that was often made in the past is to imply that certain platitudes, if applied across the board in all situations, will produce consistently high results. This simply is not true. Different circumstances require different leadership styles and behaviors. What might work in one circumstance may not necessarily work in many other, seemingly similar, circumstances.

The latest thinking in the area of leadership falls under the heading of Leadership in Context, which we touched on in an earlier chapter. Flexibility in leadership focus can be one of the most valuable traits a leader can demonstrate. One of the most substantive revelations regarding organizational leadership during the past half century has been the realization that leadership—for anyone, in any position—is practiced in five separate and distinct contexts. The five contexts are best represented using the SOTOA Model for Leadership in Context.[9]

As we examine this leadership model a little more closely, you will begin to see the road map, if you will, to becoming a stronger, more effective leader. It is in first understanding and becoming more aware of what true leadership looks like in these five contexts—and then in practicing for yourself leadership in these five contexts—that you will grow into an effective leader. So let's begin.

In the acronym SOTOA, each letter represents one of the five contexts of leadership. The S represents the Self Context, the first O represents the One-to-One Context, the T represents the Team Context, the second O represents the Organizational Context, and the A represents the Alliance Context, which is strategic in nature. Self leadership is subdivided into two sub-dimensions—understanding your core self in preparation for leadership *and* self leadership in a specific role.

---

9   Drea Zigarmi, Dick Lyles, and Susan Fowler. *Achieve Leadership Genius: How You Lead Depends on Who, What, Where, and When You Lead* (Bloomington, IN: iUniverse, 2010).

Self Context

Before we can lead effectively in any of the five contexts, it is essential that we understand ourselves. That's why the first context in which to consider leadership skills is in relationship to self. A leader must first lead himself: his inner self, his behaviors, and his habits. If you want to become a more effective leader, begin with your self leadership, your self-discipline, or, as the leadership training professionals put it: Self Context.

It's helpful to recognize that there are two subdivisions within this Self Context of leadership. The first subdivision of self leadership is to gain an understanding of our core self and how certain personal attributes affect our behavior and choices in different leadership situations. The second subdivision of self leadership is leading one's self in the context of a specific role. This involves creating a clear vision of our self in a particular role, defining key initiatives we will take to fulfill that role, assessing our own strengths and weaknesses relative to those initiatives, and developing the skills that will lead to success in that role. Each person will lead his or her self differently through different situations based on the unique attributes that he or she brings to the situation.

One-to-One Context

The key responsibility of the leader in the One-to-One Context is to develop the abilities and maximize the energy levels of each follower in order that they consistently produce excellent results for the organization. The leader's approach to each follower will vary based on each person's phase of development in their role.

Team Context

The Team Context requires the leader to effectively lead small groups, committees, task forces, or teams to the accomplishment of specific outcomes. Teams are more complicated to lead than individuals.

Organizational Context

Leading in the Organizational Context involves providing direction, structure, and processes that will align the efforts of many groups and individuals within the organization to achieve the organization's vision. Managing a series of changes is a key component of organizational leadership. The Organizational Context is the most complex. Outcomes are subjected to more variables than in any other context, and the time required to achieve organizational outcomes is generally longer than the amount required in the other contexts.

ALLIANCE CONTEXT

Alliances represent the fifth and final context. Perhaps the most significant leadership change that has taken place during the last several decades has been our shift from relying primarily on hierarchically based, unilateral energy within the organization to a reliance on networks and bilateral (two-sided, mutually beneficial) relationships that extend beyond corporate boundaries to achieve desired outcomes.

Alliances can occur on any of several levels. An alliance can be a partnership between two individuals or between an individual and an organizational unit, although these are rare. More likely alliances exist between two organizations or two organizational units. If an alliance is created between two different corporate bodies, it is an external alliance. If an alliance is created between two entities belonging to the same corporate entity, say between the marketing and sales departments of a single company, it is an internal alliance. Alliances are generally formed to accomplish long-term, mutually beneficial goals. Strategic alliances bring significant major advantage to the parties involved for an extended period of time. An example could be an alliance formed between an airline and a hotel chain to serve the ongoing needs of a certain market segment of tourists.

Within each leadership context there are four specific steps that a leader should follow. Even so, the behavior of a leader must vary within each context, depending upon the phase of performance of the followers and the specific circumstances in which the leadership is taking place.

The best place to begin learning about and mastering the concepts of leadership in context is to read *ACHIEVE LEADERSHIP GENIUS*, which I've referenced earlier. I co-authored the book with Drea Zigarmi and Susan Fowler. This is the first work to pull all the requirements of leading in context into a comprehensive, yet understandable and workable framework.[10]

If you want to thrive in your career, becoming an effective leader is essential, whether or not you want to climb the ladder of the corporate hierarchy. When I talk to people who are retired or in the autumn of their careers, the one regret I hear more than any other is that so many of them wish they had taken time out early in their careers to learn more about leadership, influencing skills, and how to adapt to others more effectively. These men and women tell me that if they'd been attentive to acquiring these skills earlier, they would have achieved more successes and more fulfillment. So take your cue from these good souls and step up to learn more about Leadership in Context now! Don't put it off. You'll see results you perhaps never thought possible!

---

10 Ibid.

36

Don't Let the Past Hold You Back

A number of NFL coaches, including Don Shula and Marty Schottenheimer, have an ironclad rule when it comes to celebrating victory or mourning their losses. After each game they allow the mourning or the celebrating to continue for twenty-four hours. No more. No less. Just twenty-four hours. Then they say it is time to move on and focus on the future.

Do these coaches forget the lessons they learned? Of course not. They recognize the value of the type of wisdom and learning that can only come from experience. Does it mean that they ignore the strengths that emerged or the weaknesses that were revealed in the previous contest? Of course not. They use the insights they gained to create strategy for future games. However, it does mean that they let go of the emotion and the excitement, the pain and the personal hurt that came with last week's game.

I'm continually amazed at the number of people who create either misery or a false sense of reality by clinging to past experiences in such a way that it prevents them from optimizing the present or the future.

Interestingly enough, this suboptimization—this severe, self-imposed limitation of one's openness to new opportunities—can result from either positive or negative experiences. Sometimes people get complacent—"fat, dumb, and happy" in the words of a long-time colleague. These people erroneously think that they can rely on yesterday's achievements to carry the load today (see Chapter 6—"*Who*

You Are Doesn't Matter"). In response to negative experiences people often get bitter and carry grudges that cloud their judgment and cause a tremendous amount of wasted energy.

I can't count the number of times I've been called in as a consultant to solve major people problems between individuals or groups. And in these situations I've listened to people tell me absolute horror stories about the people involved in the conflict, only to discover that those events happened *years* ago.

What's more amazing is that when I probe deeper to find out if anything bad has happened lately, the answer is almost always "no." They simply won't let go of the past, even when it's the past that is ruining the present, and nothing negative of significance has happened recently!

If you focus on the past, then you end up focusing on issues such as who to blame and who committed the bigger blunder. If you focus on the present and the future and let go of the past, then you end up focusing on progress, achievement, effectiveness, and success.

One reason I've been able to achieve success as a problem-solving consultant to organizations around the world is because just as soon as I work with my clients to understand the problem (what caused which undesired effects), I insist that we immediately shift focus to where we want to go from here—the future. Then we create an action plan to get there. Nothing is gained by going backward; everything can be gained by going forward.

One of my early consulting experiences proved this in spades.

A colleague phoned and explained that he had a consulting assignment that was perfectly suited to my skills and asked if I'd take it on. A friend of his named Charlie had taken over a two-billion-dollar-a-year company and he'd inherited quite a mess. The previous CEO had been concerned about the lack of cooperation and collaboration between the nineteen members of his top executive team. As near as this past CEO could tell, the problem involved all nineteen members of the team and couldn't be isolated to one specific person or a small group, so replacing one or more people wouldn't solve the problem. The predecessor had called in a psychologist to take the nineteen members away for a group retreat to iron out their differences. In preparation for the retreat, the psychologist interviewed each of the nineteen execs. Each was extremely open, recounting the many concerns and dissatisfaction each had with the other. The psychologist went back to the CEO, told him he had collected great data, and that he had more than enough information to make the weekend a success.

The CEO asked to hear some of the comments, which the psychologist willingly shared. But upon hearing the comments, the CEO went nuts. He was so angry at what his executives had openly shared with the psychologist, and he felt it was all so petty, that this former CEO decided to take matters into his own hands. He immediately called a meeting of all nineteen and proceeded to go around the room telling each person what the other people had said about him or her. The CEO went on to call people out for saying certain things about the others. He concluded by saying, "Everyone has been involved. Everyone is to blame. You're all part of the problem and this has to stop. I want everyone to knock this off as of now and get back to work. If I hear of any more of these kinds of activities in the future, I'll fire whoever is involved." Then he stormed out of the room.

The situation went from bad to worse. The group went from failure to collaborate and descended into outright dislike. They hated each other's guts, as we used to say when we were kids.

And yet none of the nineteen executives left the company! The CEO, however, took another job about six months later. It was at this point that Charlie entered the picture.

It only took Charlie about a week to discover the mess he had inherited. He was at a loss as to how to deal with it. He tried a few things that didn't work and eventually became consumed by the situation. He finally decided to schedule a weekend team-building retreat, but couldn't find anyone to conduct it.

That's when my friend called me and asked if I would conduct the retreat. I said, "No."

"Why not?" my friend asked.

"Because I'm not crazy."

My friend begged and pleaded for a while to no avail.

A week later my friend called again with the same request, and again I said I wouldn't do it.

Then a week after that he called again and asked if I'd at least agree to meet with Charlie. If I wouldn't conduct the retreat, maybe I could at least give him some advice on how to get out of the mess. I reluctantly agreed, and flew to San Francisco the next week for the meeting.

The first time I met Charlie I asked him how things were going. He said things weren't going so well. When I asked him to tell me about it, he told me about his sixteen-year-old son, having gone joyriding in his company car and blown the engine out three weeks previous, then taking the same car out joyriding two weeks previous and totaling it.

Then this past weekend his son had been smoking marijuana in his bedroom and burnt the family house down! Charlie had been traveling all over the country using any excuse to escape the challenges at home and the equally challenging environment at work. He told me that the only way he could think of to solve some of the work problems was to carry out the weekend retreat, but couldn't find anyone to conduct it. He begged me to do it.

After further discussion, I discovered that they were in the middle of their annual strategic planning process, which wasn't going smoothly.

I finally agreed to get involved and help him if—and only if—he'd do it my way. He enthusiastically agreed.

I had Charlie cancel the weekend relationship-building retreat and announce it was off the schedule forever. We then scheduled a three-day *planning* workshop to create a vision, goals, and objectives for the strategic plan. He also agreed to have me interview each executive individually before the workshop, have each of them answer a brief questionnaire, and have an afternoon meeting before the workshop to clarify expectations and discuss desired outcomes.

The interviews were a nightmare. I'd never imagined meeting nineteen people at such a high level of organizational responsibility with so much hostility toward someone they'd never even met before—me! One guy screamed and yelled at me for a full twenty minutes before I finally got him calmed down and into a somewhat reasonable conversation. Another came out from his desk, took off his tie and his shoes, then laid down on the couch in his office and said, "Okay, shrink, you've got me on the couch. Now what are you going to do to me?" One woman threw a book across her office into the wall. Another guy came around from behind his desk, sat in a side chair and rolled up his pants legs to his knees. Then he said, "Okay, what are you going to tell me?" like, I guess it's going to get pretty deep in here.

Two days of that! Two days of hostility leading to the realization that I couldn't find three people in the group who all got along with each other. In other words, for every pair of people I could find who got along, I could not find a third person who got along with them both. It was, without a doubt, the most poisoned group environment I've seen before or since.

The questionnaire I gave them asked three simple questions:

1. As a member of the executive group, what would you like to see the *planning* workshop accomplish?
2. As a member of the executive group, what criticisms do you have of *planning* methodologies that have been used in the past?
3. What would you personally like to gain from the *planning* workshop?"

I then compiled the answers to the questions and took them to the half-day meeting. I left the names off all the information so people could see the 100% positive responses without filtering the data through any personal biases. Then we went to the workshop.

The first morning we took an in-depth look at the future operating environment. The most important thing I felt I could do under the circumstances was to first get their heads into the future. The session was an eye-opener. They had been so focused on their battles with each other that many had forgotten the need to take the future seriously. Then we did an exercise focused on deciding what they'd like to achieve, avoid, and maintain (as a company) given future opportunities and challenges. We started work on a revised vision for the company.

The morning of the second day we finished the vision and outlined several key strategic thrusts. That afternoon each person began to craft a set of supporting strategic goals for each area of responsibility.

On the final day we had each group critique the goals of each of the other groups, offering help and outlining the support they could offer to help each other's goals be accomplished. We then reviewed all our work for the three days and identified the steps necessary to follow through and identify guidelines for working together to make sure everything would happen.

To close the workshop I asked each member of the group to make a comment—anything they felt was appropriate so we could bring the meeting to an honorable close. To this day my biggest regret is that I didn't have a tape recorder handy to record this final session. The comments each person made—sometimes to other individuals and sometimes to the group as a whole—were absolutely incredible. It would have been impossible to script better love messages. Comments included such statements as: "I never knew everyone else cared this much about the company," "I didn't realize so many other people had so much to offer," and "I'm genuinely excited about the possibility of working together in the future." "I can't believe we haven't been working like this all along."

When they got back to the office, the new relationships and positive attitudes carried forward because they were all built around two things: purpose and future.

So what's the moral of the story? If you live in the past or drag the past into the present, it will crowd out the future. Learn from the past, then leave it behind. The future holds the key to all your accomplishments.

AFTERWORD

Have you ever sat through the performance of a comedian who was extremely funny and provided belly laugh after belly laugh, and time after time during the performance you said to yourself, "That one was really funny. I'm going to have to remember to tell so-and-so"? And then the next day, of the hundreds of jokes and one-liners the comedian delivered, you could only remember one or two.

Many of my friends who have read PEARLS OF PERSPICACITY have said something similar. They say that every chapter was good and contained worthwhile advice, but because there was such a broad array of information, they weren't confident they would remember it all.

Here's how to solve that problem. Keep the book handy. My suggestion is that you keep it on the nightstand or table next to your bed. Then a couple of nights a week pick it up just before you go to sleep and skim through it, stopping when you find a chapter that catches your eye. A chapter might jump out because it relates to a particular problem or situation with which you're currently dealing, or it might pique your interest simply because you want to re-read that chapter to better grasp its concepts. Maintain this practice until you have truly internalized everything in the book.

There is one more request. I have no illusions that these are the only "pearls" out there. I believe there are pearls everywhere; some we recognize and some we don't. Rarely, when most people experience a perspicacious pearl, do they share it. So I'm asking that whenever you discover a pearl during your own journey through life, you share it. You can send it to me at dick@leadershiplegacies.com, and when we compile enough new pearls to publish Volume 2, we'll give you full credit for your contribution. That way everyone can share in the journey of making the perspicacity we acquire through our practical experiences more meaningful to us all.

Best wishes on your journey. I look forward to hearing from you

Dick Lyles

BIBLIOGRAPHY

Bandler, Richard, and John Grinder. *The Structure of Magic, Vols. 1 and 2.* Palo Alto, CA: Science and Behavior Books, 1975 and 1976.

Bolles, Richard Nelson. *What Color is Your Parachute?* Berkeley, CA: Ten Speed Press, 2009.

Canfield, J., and J. Switzer. *The Success Principles: How to Get from Where You Are to Where You Want to Be.* New York: HarperCollins, 2005.

McClelland, David C. "The Two Faces of Power," *Journal of International Affairs,* 24, No. 1, reprinted in *Organizational Psychology, Book of Readings,* Kolb, David A., et al. Upper Saddle River, NJ: Prentice Hall (1971).

McKean, Kevin. "Decisions, Decisions." *Discover* (June 1985): 22-31.

Zigarmi, Drea, Dick Lyles, and Susan Fowler. *Achieve Leadership Genius: How You Lead Depends on Who, What, Where, and When You Lead.* Bloomington, IN: iUniverse, 2010.